Sermons
on the Psalms

Sermons on the Psalms

BY HAROLD A. BOSLEY, Ph. D.

harper & brothers publishers
new york

Library of Congress catalog card number: 55–6781

To

J. M. POWYS SMITH

whose great learning in the Psalms
was equaled by his love for them

Contents

Contents

Preface

THE origin and nature of this book is clearly indicated by the title. It is composed of sermons which were presented as part of the regular preaching program of the First Methodist Church of Evanston, Illinois. They are presented here in the form in which they were delivered in the pulpit of that church. I have deliberately refrained from changing the spoken to the written word. As a matter of fact, it is easy to exaggerate the difference between the two. The instances where I was tempted to make a change from one to the other center more in the mechanics of transition from one line of thought to another and other forms of expression than in content itself.

I do not think of the sermon as a diluted or popularized essay, magazine article, or lecture. It has its own form—rather, it is its own form—of communication and, while related to other such forms, it is likely to lose most of its power if not its point if made over in their likeness.

Perhaps I should observe that the first sermon serves the same purpose in this book that it served in the presentation of the series to our congregation: A general introduction to the Psalter and, if possible or necessary, an awakening of interest in it as a book to read and study with renewed zeal.

These sermons were presented not as a series on successive Sundays but over a period of more than three years. They illustrate, for what it may be worth, the practice of centering attention upon some one book in the Bible for steady emphasis over a certain period of time. I have found the Psalter to be one of the richest books in the Bible—so much so that a preacher must be on his guard lest he neglect his study of other and more difficult books.

My indebtedness to many will be apparent; principally to J. M. Powys Smith, my beloved teacher of Old Testament at the Di-

vinity School of the University of Chicago, and to the several
authors and publishers who have given me permission to quote
from their publications. The biblical quotations are drawn in large
part from the King James Version and the Revised Standard
Version, with occasional uses of the American and Moffatt trans-
lations.

HAROLD A. BOSLEY

First Methodist Church
Evanston, Illinois

Sermons
on the Psalms

1

Songs From Life

▰▰▰▰▰▰▰▰▰▰▰▰▰▰▰▰▰▰▰▰▰▰▰▰▰▰▰▰▰▰▰▰▰▰▰

I

WHAT are the Psalms? A careful answer to this query will take us on a long journey through human experience; a journey that begins at the altar of private devotion, moves into the sanctuary of synagogue and church, and finally into the study of the scholar. Unless we see the Psalms in all three settings or from all three vantage points we shall not appreciate their true place in human life. If we are successful, even in measure, in the effort, we shall never again think of the Psalms as a "book" in the Bible; they will become one of our longest, steadiest, deepest looks into the depths of life.

It is well within the truth to say that the Psalter is the prayer book of the Hebrew-Christian tradition. Wherever that tradition has gone, the Psalter has become the book of private and public devotions for men. Our religious tradition is rich in other devotional literature, but none compares with the Psalter. It stands unchallenged as the supreme expression of the human spirit in search of an understanding of, and obedience to, the will of God.

The Psalter is singularly democratic. All men feel at home in it; it speaks a universal language; it ministers to a universal need; it carries a meaning that validates itself on a universal scale. Chrysostom, an influential leader in the early church, once described the centrality of the Psalms in the thought and life of early Christians in these interesting words,

If we keep vigil in the church, David comes first, last, and midst. If early in the morning, we seek for the melody of hymns, first, last, and midst is David again. If we are occupied with the funeral solem-

1

nities of the departed, if virgins sit at home and spin, David is first,
last, and midst. . . . In monasteries, amongst those holy choirs of
angelic armies, David is first, midst, and last. In the convents of virgins, where are bands of them that imitate Mary; in the deserts, where
are men crucified to this world and having their conversations with
God, first, midst, and last is he.[1]

The Psalter bridges the gap between cultures and cultural
epochs with an ease unknown by any other book. Though an
early book in terms of its formation, it is not "dated." Ancient,
medieval and modern man alike have found in it a lucid and
powerful expression of their inmost soul.

The Psalter is "above the battle" of sectarian division which
continues to shame our religious life. It is prized by Judaism and
Christianity alike. However widely apart these two may have been
thrust by claim and counterclaim in history, the Psalter continues
to be the strongest bridge uniting them. It is the heart of the
Union Hymnal of songs and prayers of the synagogue, the Bre-
viaries of the Roman Catholic Church, as well as the prayer book
of every Protestant church. The use of the Psalter in stated services of worship is customary throughout the Western world.
Orthodox, Roman Catholic and Protestant churches as well as all
Jewish synagogues agree in this. It is something to ponder in this
day of tragic and dangerous cleavages in the human family that
when men try to "talk" theology or sacraments or church government, they tend to pull apart, but when they engage in the worship of God (of which the Psalter is the supreme example), they
become as one. This would suggest that the point at which moves
toward unity should begin is none other than "the practice of the
presence of God." If this were done, the Psalter would loom even
larger in life than it now does.

The Psalms must be read and reread many times in order to
appreciate their beauty and power. They deserve to be studied
with every aid provided by scholarship in order to understand

[1] *The International Critical Commentary*, Vol. 1, *The Psalms*, by Charles A.
Briggs, Scribner's, 1906, p. xciv.

their universal appeal, their relevance to all sorts and conditions of men.

All Biblical books repay careful study, none more so than the Psalter. We are fortunate in the fact that it has been the object of the sustained study of Jewish and Christian scholars over two thousand years. A list of commentaries on the Psalms, written in many languages, is itself astounding. As we look at the Psalter through the lens of such scholarly research, its singular beauty and power will grow on us.

II

The message of the Psalms is centered in the great truths of religious faith: God, man, sin and salvation. These truths are not presented in closely reasoned logical argument—for which the average mortal is thankful! They come on the wings of song, to the cadence of great music. They burst out with a flood of luminous insight. They shout for a hearing with the driving intensity of great passion. The Psalms are like a skillful surgeon who, having gone through the skin, tissue, and bone of external events, finally lays bare the heart of religious experience itself.

The Psalms from first to last are an affirmation of profound personal faith in God. What a theologian might call the "attributes of God" blossom on every page of the Psalter: Kindness, goodness, patience, strength, dependability, righteousness, anger, judgment, understanding, tenderness, and many others. But the Psalmist is not interested in developing a doctrine of God; he is passionately determined to point out the deeds of God in the world, in life and in history. Instead of being a sober analyst, he is an excited guide who keeps tugging at our sleeves crying, "Look there! And there! And there! See what God has done; see what He is doing; see what He is about to do!" But even these deeds are of secondary importance: the activity of God in and through them is always primary. It is the string on which one shining deed after another is strung and held up for awe if not for adoration.

God is the Creator and sustainer of the world:

When I look at thy heavens, the work of thy fingers,
the moon and the stars which thou hast established . . .
[8:3]

The Mighty One, God the Lord,
speaks and summons the earth
from the rising of the sun to its setting.
[50:1]

In his hand are the depths of the earth;
the heights of the mountains are his also.
The sea is his, for he made it;
for his hands formed the dry land.
[95:4–5]

The 104th Psalm might well be called "The Hymn to the Creator":

Thou didst set the earth on its foundations,
so that it should never be shaken.
[v. 5]
Thou dost cause the grass to grow for the cattle,
And plants for man to cultivate.
[v.14]

O Lord, how manifold are thy works!
In wisdom hast thou made them all;
the earth is full of thy creatures.
[v. 24]

God maintains an active control of His creation. Drought, famine, adversity and defeat for king and subject, for people and individuals come at His bidding. An almost casual use of hyperbole brings the modern mind up short:

The voice of the Lord breaks the cedars,
the Lord breaks the cedars of Lebanon.
He makes Lebanon to skip like a calf,
and Sirion like a young wild ox.
[29:5–6]

It takes an unfettered imagination to see mountains cavorting around like young animals at play!

The Psalmist may and does complain repeatedly about the way in which God looks after creation, but he nowhere doubts that God does. In fact, the dubious prize of being a fool goes to the one who thinks "in his heart" that "there is no God." It is one thing to demand:

> Why dost thou stand afar off, O Lord?
> Why dost thou hide thyself in times of trouble?
> [10:1]

and quite another to agree with the wicked man all of whose "thoughts are, 'There is no God'" (10:4).

The Psalmist may think God unjustifiably deliberate in redressing wrong, asking, "How long, O Lord, wilt thou look on?" (35:17). He may even belabor God as well as beseech Him to settle down to business:

> Bestir thyself, and awake for my right,
> for my cause, my God and my Lord!
> [35:23]

But he never doubts that God can and will save him from his enemy.

The Psalter may not develop a doctrine of man, but it does paint as broad and as true a canvas of human nature as can be found anywhere. On it we see man at war and in peace, free and enslaved, ill and healthy, at home and in exile, rich and poor, powerful and weak, certain and doubtful, tranquil and convulsed with anger and hatred.

Not all pictures of human nature given in the Psalter are flattering. One such should be profoundly disturbing to religiously-minded folk at all times. If Theophrastus, the Greek satirist, had wished to include among his immortal character sketches one on "The Self-Righteous Man," he could have done no better than quote the 26th Psalm in its entirety. Reading it aloud, one wonders, "Just how smug can you be?" Not only was the writer invulnerable to "the slings and arrows of outrageous fortune"; he was also impervious to any help that might come to him through

critical experiences. The *spirit* of this Psalm is quite different from
that of the 23rd Psalm, though both set out to picture a soul at
peace with God. The difference between them is the vast difference between complacency on the one hand and assurance on the
other.

One of the most appealing aspects of the Psalter is its continuous personal emphasis. No other book in the Bible so reminds
us of a description Leon Bloy, contemporary French poet and
mystic, once gave of his own work: "I am simply a poor man who
seeks his God, sobbing and calling Him along all roads." Something of this shines through the Psalms. The personal pronouns
"I," "my," "thy," "we" are found throughout the Psalter. There
is nothing impersonal there.

> The Lord is my shepherd
> I shall not want
>
>   [23:1]
>
> I will observe thy statutes;
> O forsake me not utterly!
>
>   [119:8]

The Psalmist displays the entire spectrum of human emotion.
He "sees," "meditates," "delights," "weeps," "hates," "longs,"
"trusts," "walks," "melts," etc. as he seeks his way in the will of
God. That, more than anything else, explains why all men feel at
home in the Psalms. "The language of the heart" is a truly universal language, and any man upon hearing it will understand.

Sin is not glossed over in this handbook of devotion. It is a
brutal and tragic fact in human life that must be faced quite
openly. The sin of disobedience comes up for an accounting over
and over again. For sheer realism it is hard to improve upon the
candor of the 78th Psalm. It calls the "sainted" fathers

> A stubborn and rebellious generation,
>   a generation whose heart was not steadfast,
>   whose spirit was not faithful to God.
>
>   [v. 8]

But they flattered him with their mouths;
    they lied to him with their tongues.
Their heart was not steadfast toward him;
    they were not true to his covenant.

[vv. 36–37]

It is a sin to envy the evildoer, contends the Psalmist. The power, wealth, and seeming security of evil men almost trip the writer of the 73rd Psalm, but he catches his balance in time to avoid "the great transgression."

The sin of ingratitude is singled out for special attention. God will do great things for men, particularly Israel. In return they will be grateful for a while—then, they will forget it and begin to belabor God because He does not favor them as they think He should:

I hate the work of those who fall away;
    it shall not cleave to me.

[101:3]

It is hard to measure the indignation that throbs through the 106th Psalm as the writer recites the ingratitude of Israel's forefathers.

The sin of blindness comes in for caustic treatment:

Understand, O dullest of the people!
    Fools, when will you be wise?

[94:8]

Transgression speaks to the wicked
    deep in his heart;
there is no fear of God before his eyes.

[36:1]

The wicked plots against the righteous,
    and gnashes his teeth at him;
but the Lord laughs at the wicked,
    for he sees that his day is coming.

[37:12–3]

Growing out of and triumphing over sin in all its forms is the emphasis upon salvation or redemption. Sin is real, but so are the power and the love of God. In the end, they will win the battle over sin. The Psalmist recites the wonders God wrought in redeeming His people from Egypt, from the wilderness, and from a host of enemies. He tells how God conquers his own fears and doubts and sins. He is confident that God is sufficient for all things if men will but trust Him and be unafraid. Having affirmed his faith in the power of God's "right arm," the Psalmist inevitably calls for songs of rejoicing and adoration. It was no accident that the editors of the Psalter elected to close the book with a series of such hymns of ecstatic praise. They had learned well the lesson of the great Psalms in their collection.

III

An introductory word about the historical background of the Psalter may be helpful in appreciating its relevance to life. It is easy enough—and true—to say that the Psalms were struck up and out of real life. The inquiring mind wants to know more about the periods which produced them. Scholars have worked steadily at this and related problems, and their findings are beginning to fall into certain clear patterns.

The Psalms reflect the great moments and periods in Hebrew history. Most of them reached something like final form during the period between 400 B.C. and A.D. 100. Some may contain kernels of older songs, but they drew their food from, and their maturity was shaped by, the historical influence of later periods.

Some twenty of the Psalms look back to the Golden Age of David and Solomon and celebrate its glories. Thirteen reflect the experience of the Exile. Sixty come from the bitter persecution of the Persian period when Israel was under the heel of a savage oppressor. Twenty come from the period when Greeks had supplanted the Persians and the hard days of the Maccabean Kingdom had to be endured.

It is perhaps trite to observe that the great Psalms came from periods that "tried men's souls." The Psalms were used for private devotion as well as synagogue and temple worship as devout people sought strength to live in difficult days. Dr. Robert H. Pfeiffer writes,

The Psalter, in its final edition, cannot truly be understood except as a religious anthology for the reverent Jew, prepared for the purpose of stimulating that personal piety which became characteristic of the Pharisees. It is difficult to refrain from identifying the "righteous" and "sinners" among Jews with the Pharisees and Sadducees respectively, as in the Psalms of Solomon of a slightly later date, or at least with the groups out of which these two parties developed.

The Psalter is the great manifesto of the "Pious," that zealous crusading minority which succeeded in impressing its character on Judaism, even though remaining an *ecclesiola in ecclesia*—an Israel according to the spirit, surrounded by the inert mass of worldly and generally prosperous Jews. With holy indignation, these Pious denounce the "sinners," whom they regard as outcasts (cf. Ps. 139:19–22). Their ideal is a life of intimate communion with their God, in harmony with his will—a life in which simplicity of heart, faith in God, and good conduct are more essential than ritual worship and will eventually be rewarded by God. The intense emotions of these earnest souls, their longing for God's presence, their joyful faith, flaming hatred, agonizing doubts, black hours of despair, all find expression in the Psalter. This book is the voice of those humble believers whose virile hope, in spite of despair, and unyielding tenacity, in the midst of reverses, has kept Judaism alive and militant to the present day.[2]

Several collections of Psalms were made for various purposes. There is a reason to think there were several psalters in written form and in use before the effort was made to merge them in our present book. No one knows how long this took, but the task was completed before Jesus' day. The Psalter he used was essentially the one we have today. It reached its present form about A.D. 100. In this collection, the 150 Psalms of the Psalter were divided into general sections, each of which closes with the Doxology. The first Psalm is actually a prose introduction to the Psalter, and the last Psalm is a triumphant doxology for the entire book.

[2] *Introduction to the Old Testament*, Harper, 1948, p. 620.

Scholars have discovered many different kinds of Psalms in the Psalter: of penitence, of hate, of adoration, of simple faith. Two groups of Psalms had special uses in the life of ancient Israel: The Pilgrim Psalms (120–124) were chanted by pilgrims on their way to the temple. Some of these may have grown out of the chants of the exiles returning to their homeland at a much earlier date. The Hallelujah Psalms or psalms of praise constitute the second group (104, 105, 115–117, and parts of many others).

These and many other related facts deserve to be noted because they prove the close relationship between the Psalms and human experience. For five hundred years or more their songs of devotion had met a deep need of the human spirit. They became a part of Sacred Scripture, not through caprice but through demonstrated merit. They found their way into private devotion as well as public worship because they proved to be "a lamp" to our feet and "a light" to our paths—a service they stand ready to perform for anyone who will make them a part of his life.

We have it on good authority that "Literature is life." This suggests one clue to the greatness of the Psalter. It is composed of the deepest, truest, most luminous insights we have into the universal and permanently important experiences of the human spirit. As we desire to know ourself, our neighbor and God we shall seek the Psalmist as a daily guide and companion. Under his teaching the scales will fall from our eyes and "every common bush" will be "afire with God."

II

Strange Delight

~~~~~~

SCRIPTURE LESSON: Psalm 1

I

WE ARE so familiar with the first Psalm that it is difficult to appreciate the full force of its abrupt challenge. Yet, if we will study it for a moment, then study ourselves in the light of it, we shall see the sharp line it draws across our life as it lifts the ancient challenge: Choose ye this day!

Strange as it may seem, the first Psalm was the last psalm to be written. Late in Hebrew history the scribes of the Temple in Jerusalem were editing the psalter, the hymbook of the Temple. They thought, quite naturally, that the new edition ought to have some kind of introduction. The hundred and more Psalms dealt with many themes and, to a casual reader, might seem to be teaching different lessons upon occasion. Believing as they did that certain great motifs dominated the Psalms, the scholars (whether one or many, we have no way of knowing) wrote the first Psalm as the needed introduction. In it, they singled out these motifs and presented them as the outstanding teachings of the entire psalter. The result is the literary and spiritual gem most of us learned in childhood, the cadences of which we have never forgotten.

The structure of the Psalm is simplicity itself. It states and sharpens up the contrast between the godly and the ungodly man. Or as we would say, between the religious and the irreligious man. As we well recall, the ungodly man has a rough time of it, coming off a poor second in this comparison. He is like the "chaff that the

11

storm carrieth away." Yet it would be a mistake for us to assume that the godly, the religious man, has an easy time of it. That, surely, is not the teaching of the psalter, nor is it even so much as suggested by the first Psalm.

He who would know the favor, the protection, and the joy of God, he who would be blessed, as the Psalmist uses the word, is confronted with the sharp insistence that there are some things he must do and others he must not do. He must not walk "in the counsel of the ungodly," or stand "in the way of sinners," or sit "in the seat of the scornful." Or as we would say, he must avoid irreligious counselors; he must avoid the companionship of those who openly and knowingly disobey God; he must not join company with those who are cynical and skeptical about God, who say in their heart, "There is no God."

Affirmatively, "his delight is in the law of the Lord; and in his law doth he meditate day and night." He must do more than passively accept the law of the Lord. That, conceivably, might be done with a wail of self-pity or even with a howl of outraged righteousness. He might accept the law of the Lord as a convicted criminal accepts the fact that he is about to be sentenced by a judge. Which attitude, I suspect, is of a piece with the defiant acquiescence of a small boy who said of the medicine his father was bringing, "I have to take it, but I don't have to like it, do I?" The Psalmist holds that the blessed man will have a quite different attitude toward the Law of God: he will make it the object of joyous contemplation at all times; he will delight in it.

This, to our generation, must seem a strange delight. For law, to us, is not so much a delight as a sorrow. Law restricts, denies, inhibits and compels us—and we object to such disciplining. A. E. Housman has given almost perfect expression to our rebellious mood in his famous lines:

> The laws of God, the laws of man,
> He may keep that will and can;
> Not I; let God and man decree

Laws for themselves and not for me;
And if my ways are not as theirs
Let them mind their own affairs.[1]

Before we attempt to decide between the strange delight of the Psalmist and the truculence of our contemporaries on this matter, I suggest that we look with some care into the general relationship between law and life. This is precisely what the Psalmist did before he reached the conclusion that brings us up so sharply. He had spread out before him, as it were, not only a thousand years of Hebrew history recorded in tradition, legend and sacred writings, but, in addition, he had the reflections, insights and judgments of the prophets, priests and poets who had preceded him. So far from being a lonely mystic isolated on some mountaintop, the Psalmist was gazing intently at what had been going on in human life and history as he proclaimed his delight in the law of the Lord.

II

This law of the Lord in which he delighted was no simple, single event; it was a broad all-inclusive thing, meaning, in fact, three different though closely related events or experiences. We need do little more than note them now in order to grasp the majestic importance of their meaning.

First, then, the law of God indicates the order of creation, the orderliness of the universe. The tradition of the creation of all things by God is one of the most firmly grounded convictions of ancient Israel. This universe is no chance affair; it was created by God for His purpose and through His will and power. The actual order of the world, then, is itself the creation of God. The poets of ancient Israel never tired of singing of the glory of God's world: "When I consider thy heavens, the work of thy fingers, the moon and the stars, which thou hast ordained . . ." "The heavens declare the glory of God; and the firmament showeth his handiwork."

[1] From *The Collected Poems of A. E. Housman.* Copyright, 1940, by Henry Holt and Company, Inc. Reprinted by permission of the publishers, and of the Society of Authors, London, England.

For the Psalmist, man is no outsider in God's world; he belongs to the order of creation. Actually, he checks in at the very top of that order—a fact that reduces the Psalmist to an acute condition of anxious awe:

> What is man that thou art mindful
>   of him. . . .
> For thou hast made him a little lower
>   than the angels,
>   and hast crowned him with glory
>   and honour.
> Thou madest him to have dominion over
>   the works of thy hands;
>   thou hast put all things under his
>   feet.
>   [8:4-6]

God has had and keeps a personal eye on man from the beginning: Before he was born, wherever he goes. Lest man begin to strut about in his singular glory, the Psalmist makes it plain that he is not celebrating an idle favor which God has conferred upon man; he is calling attention to two searching facts: (1) man is no chance being; he is a child of God, created in His image; (2) life is a stewardship, a divine trust that must be accepted as a gift from God and accounted for in the presence of God Himself.

The second broad fact which enters into the meaning of the law of the Lord in which the Psalmist delights is the reality of Providence in human life and history. Keenly aware of the reality of God in the order of creation, he is even more acutely conscious of the presence and purpose of God in history. Like all Hebrews, he regards history as the medium through which God deals directly with men. He believes that the punishment of the ungodly man and the reward of the godly man are to be found to some extent in history.

Like the Psalmist, the prophets of ancient Israel were firm believers in Providence, in the will and the power of God in life and history. This conviction was the vantage point from which they

studied the history of their own people. It was the firm foundation
on which they stood as they brought them before the bar of divine
judgment. History, they thought, is not immoral or amoral; it is
spiritual and moral through and through because God is at its
heart. They were not foolish enough to believe for one moment
that history is all good. They did believe that the goodness and the
power of God are in it, trying to find expression in all that men say
and do.

The third fact which composed the Law of the Lord to which
the Psalmist calls attention is the actual expression of His will in
the Law book, the Torah and the Pentateuch—the first five books
of our Bible. This the good Jew held to be the revelation of the
will of God for the Hebrew people. While they might differ on
how literally to take its teachings, they agreed that it was God's
covenant with them. One of the truly distinctive things about the
life and culture of Israel is this conviction that they are a Holy
People and have been given a Holy Land in which, and a Holy
Law by which, to live.

The Psalmist was letting his eye range over these broad facts of
human experience, then, when he said: "Blessed is the man
[whose] delight is in the law of the Lord; and in his law doth he
meditate day and night."

III

Though the Psalmist set down this expression of faith two thousand years ago, his delight in the law of the Lord has not been dis-
owned by subsequent generations. It has stood the test of time.
And what a testing it has been given! Generation after generation
of skeptical, cynical and proud peoples have turned away from it
with a sneer, thinking to ignore it forever, only to grope their way
back to it, blinded by the tragedy that eternally and irrevocably
attends human folly. Many of the most powerful thinkers of our
own time, whose interests lie quite outside the professions of the
ministry or the church, are inclined to agree with the Psalmist's
faith in the law of God.

The scientist, better than anyone else, knows that we live in a cosmos not a chaos, knows that we live in an essentially orderly universe. Emil Myerson, himself one of the great philosophers of science of our time, may have been stretching it a bit, some will think, when he said, "Never has any scientist worthy of the name doubted that nature, even in its most intimate recesses, was entirely subject to law." If so, he has the strong support of half a dozen of the most prominent scientists in this country whose testament of faith appeared a few years ago in a little booklet entitled *My Faith.*

Dr. Kirtley Mather says flatly, "We live in a universe, not of chance or caprice, but of law and order." And when Dr. Albert Einstein writes, "Certain it is that a conviction, akin to religious feeling, of the rationality or intelligibility of the world lies behind all scientific work of a higher order," his colleagues are in complete agreement. Sir James Jeans summarizes the testament of science in this telling way: "We discover that the Universe shows evidence of a designing or controlling power that has something in common with our own individual minds."

Sometimes these giant intellects seem to be a little lacking in charity because they are not at all gentle in their treatment of skeptics. Plato is one who found it hard to keep calm in the presence of one who doubted the existence of the gods. "How can anyone in gentle terms remonstrate with the like of them?" he demands to know. He contends that "the reality of the gods would be admitted by all who had any particle of intelligence."

That, I fear, is taking it to the extreme, though the matter of the order of the universe might well be left where one of our own philosophers, Professor F. J. E. Woodbridge, places it: "To regard nature as the symbol of God's glory is not at all strange or unnatural. It is very human. It is, perhaps, the thing we are ultimately led to do when, thoroughly sophisticated, disillusioned, and disenchanted, we take ourselves seriously in hand and ask what is our business here. Then we stand confronted by the Ancient of Days."

Dr. Herbert Butterfield, professor of modern history at Cambridge University, startles us with his sharp insistence that the only intelligible clue to history is to be found in the idea of the Provi-

dence of God. This, he contends, was the secret of the success of
the Hebrew prophet's approach to history. He holds, throughout
his book, *Christianity and History*, that even the professional historian will get lost in his data unless he has, as a vantage point,
some such guiding idea from which to get his sense of direction.

Actually, the cardinal sin of history makers and history writers
over the last four hundred years was wrapped up in the conceited
utterance of one of our radio commentators a few years ago: "History is what we make it; we can make it what we will." The vastly
different contention of historic religion is that history is what God
permits us to make it. History is the medium through which God
deals with us—deals, not as a billiard player cues the balls on a
cosmic table, but as a father deals with his children. Once let convictions like these get abroad in the minds of men and nations and
a new dimension of responsibility before God will become at least
as real as responsibility before man.

I myself am sure the Psalmist had a good point when he delighted in the spiritual and moral heritage of his own faith and
people. How can we avoid paying tribute to the indestructible
power of that kind of heritage? It alone explains the history of the
Jewish people: their sense of destiny and purpose in history; their
unconquerable hope and faith in the presence of the worst of
man's inhumanity to man. Nothing less than the faith that they
were under the shadow of His wings could have sustained them.

After we, in our own time and tradition, have tired of the rather
cheap sport of making fun of our Puritan fathers and of disasso-
ciating ourselves from every lingering taint or tinge of Puritanism
lest we be regarded as soft-headed—we, if we are simply honest
with the known facts of American thought and life, will pay tribute
to the solid spiritual strength which that tradition has given our
way of life. Even when we have ignored it, we have depended upon
the ethical ideals and institutions which it created. Even when we
have renounced it, we have tried to retain and keep alive by various sorts of forced feedings and hothouse procedures its convictions about the dignity, worth and ethical responsibility of man.

Most emphatically, we are not in the position of the Ozark

mountaineer who, when accused of a crime, was being interviewed by a social worker assigned to the case by the court. The social worker, discovering that the man could neither read nor write, asked, "Why didn't your parents teach you how to read and write?" The man replied, "Mister, ye can't give what ye hain't got, any more'n ye can go back where ye never been!" We have a great spiritual heritage that we now are trying to get back to—and it is high time.

The encouraging action of the State Board of Regents of New York in 1953 indicates how serious we are about recovering our sense of dependency on our spiritual heritage.

This Board, as you may know, sets the policies for the public school system of New York State. Consequently, what it says not only arises from practical experience but must also deal directly with practical problems. Troubled by the charge and the fact of secularism and irreligion in the public schools, they were trying to bring about a rebirth of concern for, and knowledge of, our spiritual inheritance. They did so in a short document which has since become a classic—and a trail blazer of policy in other states. These sentences from it give us the spirit of the entire document:

Belief in and dependence upon Almighty God was the very corner-stone upon which our Founding Fathers builded. Our State Constitution opens with these solemn words: "We, the people of the State of New York, grateful to Almighty God for our freedom, in order to secure its blessings, do establish this Constitution." We are convinced that this fundamental belief and dependence of the American—always a religious people—is the best security against the danger of these difficult days. In our opinion, the securing of the peace and safety of our country and our state against such dangers, points to the essentiality of teaching our children, as set forth in the Declaration of Independence, that Almighty God is their Creator, and that by him they have been endowed with their inalienable rights of life, liberty and the pursuit of happiness.

We believe that at the commencement of each school day the act of allegiance to the flag might well be joined with this act of reverence to God: "Almighty God, we acknowledge our dependence upon thee, and we beg thy blessings upon us, our parents, our teachers and our country." We believe that the school day thus started might well include specific programs stressing the moral and spiritual heritage which is America's, the trust which our pioneering ancestors placed in Almighty God, their gratitude to him from whom they freely and frequently acknowledged came their blessings and their freedom and their abiding belief in the free way of life and in the universal brotherhood of man based upon their acknowledgment of their Creator, Almighty God, whom they loved and reverenced in diverse ways.

The State Board closes this remarkable document by recording its conviction that some such recentering of emphasis upon the spiritual heritage of this country will make us a more unified and law-abiding people and bring about a renewal of devotion to high moral standards.

Like the Psalmist we may yet learn to delight in our moral and spiritual heritage of reverence for the law of the Lord.

IV.

But there are those among us who object to the idea of external law, whether human or divine. They think it an invasion of their freedom and would agree with Gutzon Borglum, the sculptor, "Laws are for those that need them—I don't!" Before we mount that toboggan slide to sheer tragedy we ought to reflect on the fact that law is positive as well as negative. It not only denies, it grants; it not only takes away, it gives. Actually, the positive implications of the law of the Lord which we are studying can be summed up in two brief commandments. As we look at them, we shall see that it is the part of good sense not only to accept the law, but to delight in it as well.

The first one can be phrased quite simply: *Thou shalt think God's thoughts after Him.*

This commandment is hard for some of us to take. It demands that we get out of the limbo of ideas without action, of words without deeds. It demands that we approach life not as a potter approaches clay, able to mold it however he wills, but as one person approaches another in the spirit of understanding and co-operation. It demands, in short, that we view life as a thoroughly responsible ethical business. Some of us are repelled by this approach. We are inclined to agree with the criticism the editorial writer of the student paper of a large university once made of a Religious Emphasis week program on that campus. It was too evangelical, he said. It tried to get students to make commitments, to embrace specific positions. That was taking it too far, he argued. He wanted to talk about truth but not about religion, about values but not about God, about human relationships but not about human nature. Obviously we cannot have it both ways, and the sooner we find it out the better for all concerned. Any significant discussion about the great values of truth, beauty, goodness and love soon finds its way up to the high level of the mystery of the Law of the Lord of Life.

Still others among us reject the notion that there is anything ultimate or absolute about these great values; we want to feel that they are relative, through and through. Hitler belonged to this group. He once assured his fellow nihilists, "The Ten Commandments have lost their validity. There is no such thing as truth, either in the moral or in the scientific sense." Believe that, and truth becomes a convention rather than a conviction. It becomes the tool of governments, or of the majority, or of some institution or other. It is no longer the basis on which a man may appeal against the government, or against the majority, or against an institution.

When that view of truth prevails (God forbid it ever should) a good many more things than the Ten Commandments will lose their validity. Democracy will disappear forthwith because it must recognize the right of the individual to differ from the group. It must actually prize the fact that the individual will differ from the group, or it becomes some form of collectivism. Science and art will have hard sledding in that evil day when man is the measure of all things, when the reality of the Law of God ceases to be a vital factor in our thought and life. When the scientist searches for the answer to a problem he must believe that he is looking for something that is actually there or he is foolish to conduct the search. If he believes that an answer can be found and therefore should be sought, he is standing, whether consciously or not, in the great tradition of those who delight in the law of the Lord.

Every great artist is keenly aware of the fact that he is an explorer in and an interpreter of the work of the great Artist Himself. Gamaliel Bradford was beautifully explicit: "Without God, the whole universe crumbles." And indeed it does. But with God, it surrounds us as a thing of infinite mystery yet our home, unknown in its vast outreaches yet knowable in so many ways, bristling with a hundred tragic problems to which man has not found the answer, yet in every fundamental movement friendly to man. It is the prime business of man to dedicate himself to the task of thinking God's thoughts after him if he would explore the mysteries of the universe and his own life. But he must do so in a thoroughly responsible manner. He must not be like the eloquent Negro preacher who concluded his prayer of dedication with this petition: "O Lord, use me! Use me! Especially in an advisory capacity."

Thou shalt think God's thoughts after Him: believe this, and at a stroke, you become a committed person—committed to the conviction that you must seek truth, beauty, goodness and love wherever they may be found because they are of God, because they are God's hand on man's shoulder leading him toward the abundant life. You will know that any and every effort to sever their meaning and content from God is false and must be renounced. You will rejoice in the unseverable relationship which exists between these values that are so precious to human life and the Lord of Life Himself.

Believe in the reality of the Law of the Lord, and you will be led to a second commandment: *Thou shalt love God and man utterly.* Easy to say but hard to do, isn't it? Most of us feel that a good many things have to be cleared up about both God and man before we can actually love them.

There are times when we may even feel as Clarence Day said his father seemed to feel in his praying: "He didn't actually accuse God of gross inefficiency, but when he prayed, his tone was loud and angry, like that of a dissatisfied guest in a carelessly managed hotel." But in our better moments we know that the weight of evidence is all on the side of a far different attitude toward the Creator of the universe and of the other members of the human family. It is a positive attitude, one which great religion suggests as humility, trust and devotion. This attitude does more than merely accept the universe, as Margaret Fuller did; it accepts it with joy and proposes to find the way of human life in the will of God, the Father of all men. It is a venture of faith, to be sure, but not a blind venture. It is the rational, sensible conclusion to be drawn from the fact of God in the world.

The Christian faith, believing that God is love, urges us to try to be fit instruments of His holy will in our daily life. Browning was true to the Christian understanding of love when he said, "All's love yet all's law." The law of which we speak and in which we believe is not mechanical but moral; it is not a matter of routine, but of divine love. What God did and does by and through law was and is done with purpose and love and is fashioned from a sincere desire that men would know and understand the will of God. Man is no automaton, but a child—a child of God—a free moral agent to whom God must make a personal approach and a moral appeal. But, in the end, God must be God even as a father must be a father. When God disciplines man through denial or sacrifice, even tragedy, it is not because God wants it that way but because men leave Him no other avenue through which He can proceed. Man has real freedom relative to the will of God; he can block God partially, but never wholly. God cannot command and coerce the understanding and the love of man, but He can seek it and try to get men to give it in love and faith. He can seek it as a teacher seeks confidence of a pupil or a father seeks love and understanding of a son.

This much seems to be clear about the law of God. We cannot break it, but we can break ourselves upon it. We can disobey it, but we cannot escape it. It is the literal Hound of Heaven to one who seeks to escape it. But to one who accepts and obeys it with joy in his soul it is indeed a strange delight. It means strength, peace, joy. It enables him to say:

The Lord is my shepherd, I
   shall not want. . . .
Yea, though I walk through
   the valley of the shadow of death,
 I will fear no evil:
for thou art with me;
   thy rod and thy staff
   they comfort me. . . .
Surely goodness and mercy shall
    follow me
   all the days of my life;
and I will dwell in the house of
    the Lord
   forever.

III

The Appetite of Iniquity

SCRIPTURE LESSON: Psalm 14

I

HISTORIC religion has learned many things in the course of her long journey since the dawn of the human enterprise. She has learned them the hard way, and she has been forced to test them over and over again in the one place where every idea and insight is declared to be either important or unimportant—namely, the crucible of human experience. Not the experience merely of this person or that, this age and people or that age and people, but the experience of all men who have been exposed to the idea and insight over the ages. People who say or infer that religion is the creation of either fear-ridden men or wishful thinkers or utopian dreamers, usually overlook this fact as they frame their superficial indictment. If they would only center their attention for a while upon what religion has learned, created and achieved in human history, they would be in a much stronger position to make a fair estimate of her worth. And if they would look carefully at the facts, they would discover high on the scale of important lessons she has learned one that is especially relevant to our times: *the meaning and the power of evil in life must be faced openly and overcome honestly by all who seriously want to bring their lives to any kind of fulfillment.* This lesson was hammered out on the anvil of individual as well as group experience. It has been checked and rechecked by the experience of many generations—each of which has had its quota of skeptics and cynics about this whole business of

24

ethics, morals and religion. It comes as close to being a completely demonstrated fact as we can possibly hope to get from history. And yet—we are living witnesses to the ancient truth that "the one thing we learn from history is that we do not learn from history."

We are dodging and twisting every way today in our frantic efforts to evade the meaning and the power of evil in our individual and corporate life. We shrink from any serious use of the words "sin" and "iniquity." They grate on our ears; they jar our sensitivities; they disturb our aplomb; we quickly charge them off as the tools of fanatics, and go thankfully but apprehensively on our way, hoping to hear no more about them. Yet we can no more escape them than Francis Thompson could forever elude "The Hound of Heaven." The facts denoted by the words "sin" and "iniquity" are a living part of our own life. Wherever we look—whether inside us or round about us—we see the facts of sin and iniquity writing their tragic lessons in the pain, suffering and tragedy of lives and times like ours. Look carefully at any great issue before men today, and we will discover facts there that our fathers before us would have designated unhesitatingly as sin and iniquity. Earlier religious thinkers may have missed some facts about human life, but they did not miss the fact of sin—nor did they mistake what one of them truly called "the gravity of sin."

The writer of the 14th Psalm gives us a sharp description of what might well be called the appetite of iniquity. He both appreciated the gravity of sin and was certain he lived among a people who did not. All this and more, too, shines through his description of sinners as those "who eat up my people as they eat bread." He laid his finger on the root cause of sin in their life, and he pointed it out to all who would listen.

Sin, the Psalmist says, stems from the effort to ignore or deny God. People who think this way are led along the pathway of disaster by the delusion that they are on their own, that they are entitled to do whatever they want to do and are strong enough actually to do. Sin, he continues, is never abstract or academic; it is tragically personal and human. It is not a static something or other; it is truly demonic in nature. It preys on persons and personal relationships, on values and virtues. And of its appetite there is no end. Sin is the perfect answer to a conundrum that used to be circulated in the rural school I attended as a boy. We would say, "I'm thinking of something: the more it eats the more it wants." The answer we sought and usually got was "the threshing machine," but the Psalmist would have given a different answer: "sin" or "iniquity."

Subsequent thinkers in our religious tradition have been in complete agreement with the Psalmist's judgment on sin. Calling it, as he did, woeful disobedience to God, they both enlarged upon its many forms in life and conjured up vivid pictures of the various kinds of punishment in store for various kinds of sin. We may discount the details of Dante's *Inferno* if we will—and none can say us nay as we do it—but we dare not discredit either the reality of sin or the inevitability of punishment of some sort for it. "Why not?" you ask. And the reply can be brief: *Our soul is at stake.*

This view of the gravity of sin is coextensive with the Christian faith. From Paul's day to our own, it has been a fixed point of reference in the thought of every religious thinker. Martin Luther quotes with complete approval an early Latin churchman's clear picture of the ruin sin makes in life: "The spirit of man is compassed about and besieged by the assaults of the devil and can hardly meet, hardly withstand them all. If avarice is overthrown, lust rises; if lust is put down, ambition takes its place; if ambition is displaced, then anger grows bitter, pride puffs itself up, drunkenness assails, hatred breaks the bonds of concord, envy destroys friendship. . . ."

John Calvin was equally gloomy about the dynamic nature of iniquity: "Infidelity opened the gates to ambition, and ambition produced obstinacy, so that they cast off the fear of God and precipitated themselves whithersoever they were led by their lawless desires. . . . Man has not only been ensnared by the inferior appetites, but abominable impiety has seized the very citadel of his mind, and pride has penetrated into the inmost recesses of his heart." Study that picture of man's plight, and you will appreciate

Dr. Paul Scherer's remark, "Calvin couldn't stop sin, but he could take all of the fun out of it."

II

Biblical and later religious writers are not alone in their perception of this insatiable appetite of iniquity. The great Greek tragedians had an almost terrifying sense of the implacable reality of it and the punishments that attend it. They personified it as "the Furies" who harassed the sinner to the point of death and even beyond death as he sought and was denied the peace of the Elysian fields. Small wonder, then, that Sophocles closed his greatest play, Oedipus, King of Thebes,[1] with the somber warning:

> Therefore, O man, beware, and look toward
>   the end of things that be,
> The last of sights, the last of days; and no
>   man's life account as gain
> Ere the full tale be finished and the darkness
>   find him without pain.

Shakespeare was a past master at depicting the relentless growth of evil in the life of a man until it literally took possession of him. List his heroes: Othello, Macbeth, Hamlet, Caesar, Brutus and Mark Antony, and in every case one can trace the swift corruption of mind, motive and relationships that builds toward the tragic climax of each play.

In our own time Eugene O'Neill has been peculiarly sensitive to the same tragic reality in human life. A student of his dramas once observed that, for O'Neill, the quest was always for God. This, I am sure, is true—and the reason why God is the ultimate goal of his quest is the keen perception which he shares with the Psalmist that, without God, life is engulfed in wickedness.

No novelist has dipped so deeply into the malignant meaning of evil in human life as has Dostoevski. All of his novels have this as a characteristic motif. He is appallingly specific about the circumstances under which it takes root in one's life: atheism, agnosti-

---

[1] Translated by Gilbert Murray. Copyright, 1911, by Oxford University Press, 1939, by Gilbert Murray. Reprinted by permission of the publisher.

cism and skepticism. Let a man find himself in a situation in which he has lost the inner spiritual guards of faith—and his soul is forfeit forthwith. Sin and evil move in and take over, and he is hurled to an awful fate. The only possible way to break the power of evil is through the recommitment of oneself to God, thereby finding the spiritual strength to resist evil successfully.

It is idle to hope to add much, if anything, of consequence to these master draftsmen of the workings of the human spirit when caught in the throes of iniquity, but I would like to single out for special attention one fact that they all assume or imply. The final movement in the expansion of the appetite of iniquity is this: Sin wants to pass for righteousness; vice masquerades as virtue; the devil lusts for sainthood! Actually, of course, this represents the ultimate triumph open to evil—to be mistaken for good. Every sin that corrupts life tries to do that very thing. Thus Milton has his Satan cry out, "Evil, be thou my good!"

III

Manifestly, so great an array of novelists, dramatists, poets and seers would not concern themselves with the ravages of iniquity in life if it were not a universal fact and problem. We are, then, justified in asserting that iniquity is an ever-present personal fact, that no man can escape it, that every man must learn how to cope with it.

It was Jesus himself who saw that no man is good enough to be called or to be regarded or to feel himself as completely good. When someone addressed him as "Good Master," Jesus interrupted, "Why callest thou me good? There is none good but one— even God." He never by so much as one word let his disciples think that they were beyond the contagion of iniquity. He knew and said and bequeathed to his Church the keen awareness that the seeds of evil and corruption lie deep within the lives of all and are always trying to break through into the sunlight of approval and opportunity to grow and bear their tragic fruit in life.

We do not need to stir out of our own company this morning to document this ancient Christian claim. It will take a longer sheet of paper than the mind of men can conceive to record the evil that good men have done and continue to do in the name of goodness!

The Jews who stoned the prophets were good men; that is, men who believed that in protecting the status quo they were doing the works of good men. The men who were all for stoning the woman taken in adultery were the very custodians of the codes of high personal and social morality—codes they were sworn to defend with their own lives. When Saul of Tarsus assisted the selfsame custodians of traditional religion in killing Stephen, both he and they felt that they were good men and had done a good day's work. Cotton Mather, New England divine in early Colonial days, was a good man by any fair standard of measurement, yet for hardness of heart and merciless probity of spirit he had few equals. Even those who acclaimed him a good man hated to have him around because the milk of human kindness had never been a part of his diet. When Hermann Hagedorn wrote his tremendous poem, *The Bomb That Fell on America*,[2] he cast most of it in terms of a dialogue between God and the one who cried:

> I'm a good man, Lord! . . .
> I'm one of your troopers . . . Lord, I've been
> fighting your battles
> For years and years, a lifetime, in fact, you
> might say.
> On the side of the angels, I put it, always on
> the side of the angels.

I am not making fun of these people. They were all good people whose goodness had gone sour. And the souring process is pretty much the same in every case. They were proud of their goodness; they gloried in it; they were not above boasting about it; they even measured other people against it in order to determine their worth. In so doing, they let loose in their lives the sin of pride. Whatever else pride does, it blinds a man to the worth of everything at variance with what he holds to be good; it nurtures a kind of self-

righteousness that makes rationalizations easy and easy to believe.
Unrebuked by a humility born of an awareness of the greatness,
the glory and the mercy of God, pride takes over the reins of a
man's life and drives him to his own ruin. No truer line was ever
penned than this: "Pride goeth before a fall."

This corruption of goodness, whether through pride or lust or
greed, is so close to each one of us, so human, so unavoidable! It
can and it will happen in some measure to everyone here. We
may not be as obvious as was the Kansas farmer whose holdings
were enormous, but who, when accused of being greedy, answered,
"I'm not greedy. I just want all the land that joins mine." Without
realizing it, he touched off the temptation that lies at the heart of
what Justice Brandeis was fond of calling "the danger of bigness"
in modern industry. Justice Brandeis objected to monopolies of
every kind whether the closed shop for labor or great business
aggregates that stifle competition. When he spoke of "the tyranny
of capital" industrialists called him a socialist; when he spoke of
"the tyranny of labor" labor leaders called him a tool of capitalism.
But he is better regarded as a sincere social prophet who knew the
reality and power of the appetite of iniquity in human life. In case
after case he hammered home the truth that the desire to own
everything that joins yours contains the seeds of an evil that for all
its good fruits along the way will finally shower the bitter fruits of
tragedy on men and social orders.

All of which appears to confirm Carlyle's notoriously dim view
of human nature. Many of you will recall his belief that if you
think you can make a poor bootblack happy by giving him things
you are doomed to disappointment. Give him half the world, and
he will grieve himself to death because he doesn't have the other
half! The desire for possession is both good and normal, but couple
it with the conviction that you are answerable to yourself alone—
not to God; not even to other men—and it suddenly becomes the
evil of greed or avarice or covetousness. And, as Carlyle saw, there
is no satisfying the appetite of that iniquity.

And let us never forget that an evil on the loose in life never
confesses its true nature; it always masquerades as good. Prejudice

—racial prejudice—is an excellent example of how this operates. It begins with the fact of differences between and among races. Whether these differences are relative or absolute is irrelevant for the moment. It proceeds with the fact that as a rule racial groups prefer to live together—at least, that is the history of mankind to date. It calls attention to various differences in culture, education and ability which are thought to exist among racial groups. It points out that a social order ought to make provision for these differences and preferences in its conventions, laws and zoning ordinances. It calls this line of reasoning realistic and argues that it serves the best interests of all.

This, of course, is a very genial presentation of the bitter fact of prejudice. If you want it translated into realistic terms, you must talk about certain tendencies in Evanston; you must talk about Cicero and South Africa. Whenever prejudice presents itself as good custom and stable convention, know it for a fact that iniquity is parading in the garments of holiness, and may even have persuaded itself that it is holy.

We live at a time when still another evil is threatening to take over the lives of a great many of us. You can call it by many names. The one that seems to me to be truest to its nature is simply "passion"—in one of several concrete forms. Note two of these—hatred and sexual license. Both are uncriticized and uncontrolled products of normal human passions. Each roots in something that is good, yet which, in full flower, showers tragedy and ruin on all.

Hatred of another country, say, springs basically from love of one's own and fear for her welfare and future. We love her so much that we love her too much. We set her above other countries; we not only desire her welfare, we desire it more than the welfare of others. And this state of mind always winds up with our desiring her welfare above and beyond the welfare of anyone else and, if need be, at the expense of other countries. Having no view of the human family that is comprehensive and compassionate enough to see all men as essential and integral parts of it, we begin by loving our country and end by hating every other country that seems to be at variance with, or standing in the way of, what we want to do for her.

Oh, we seldom put it just that way, do we? We rationalize it beautifully, and when we are through, the appetite of iniquity has been enlarged to the point that evil appears as a good, and we have made the worse appear the better cause.

Sexual license or the uncriticized and uncontrolled gratification of the sexual interest and instinct in life follows the same general pattern. No one suddenly says, "Go to, now. I am going to have a sex instinct." You and everyone else are born with that. Seen as an essential part of one's life but not the whole of it, treasured as a healthy factor in the unfoldment of one's life and relationships, it is good in every sense of that term. But let it get out of control of this over-all picture of its proper place in life, and it rapidly takes over as the dominant factor in living. When that happens, you get a stream of lurid sexy pictures, books and plays that both spring from and pander to sexual license or the sex instinct on the loose. Sex interests, pleasures and acts become ends in themselves and develop cults that accept them as the great goods of life. D. H. Lawrence may well be regarded as the High Priest of the Cult of Sexual License that has been attracting and continues to attract so many devotees to its orgiastic rites. Read his novels, *Sons and Lovers* or *Lady Chatterly's Lover*, and you get a serious, studious presentation of the case of sexual license as the most important thing in the world. But open any daily paper with its headlines of rape and perversion, and you get some of the grim results of this preachment let loose in life. We have not yet found any way to nurture a normal human personality or to create stable marriages and homes or to be capable dependable parents unless we keep the sex instinct under the higher loyalty of what life can and ought to mean.

IV

Nor is this lesson about the appetite of iniquity confined to the evils that bedevil individuals. Every institution as well as every person must face it in some form or other.

For more than four hundred years now nations in this modern era have been trying to achieve enough power to feel secure. Who can quarrel with that objective? Surely it is the minimum responsibility of government to provide for the security of its people. Thus reasoned the kings who thought themselves divinely ordained to positions of authority. Thus reasoned the revolutionaries who sought to overthrow them in the name of the people's rights. Thus reason the leaders in Soviet Russia, in China, in England and in the United States today. Reasoning thus, the stage is laid for the kind of conflicts that have opened the arteries of Europe, if not of the world, over the past one hundred and fifty years.

The two great antagonists on the stage just now are, as we all know, the Soviet Union and our own country. Neither is sure it can live in the same world with the other; the leaders of both countries blow hot and cold on that possibility. Neither trusts the other's intentions in world politics, and both are frantically trying to build up enough power to guarantee security to their own people. Like the Kansas farmer, each protests that it is not imperialistic; it just wants to be sure of the politics of each nation that lies on its borders or close to some of the sources of its necessities of life. Neither has yet had a vision of security on a broad enough scale to make the other feel at ease, and present leaders of both countries have demonstrated their inability to construct such a vision. Lacking it, each country continues to define security in terms of its ability to control increasing sections of this world's people and resources. Each protests either its innocence or at least its peaceful intentions as it expands, but once committed to what amounts to a program of world control, if not domination, the evil of expansion grows by leaps and bounds. We expand the area of our financial and military commitments to the very ends of the earth. There is good reason to believe that Russia has done likewise. We build up a vast military machine—as does Russia. The race for security now under way, if not checked, is fated to end either in mutual destruction in war or in the bankruptcy of both social orders in the effort to be strong enough to keep peace. Yet the evil of expansion through domination parades as good sense, as realism, as steps toward peace. I have even heard it presented as the solution which Christian ethics advocates in terms of this world situation! Here again we see vice parading in the soiled robes of virtue. And one must be hopelessly blind not to see the end of it all—unless we recognize the deceiver and call him by his name. If we keep on calling evil good, the end will be that we are consumed by the appetite of iniquity.

The Christian Church is not above the ravages of this appetite of iniquity. Examples of it exist in embarrassing profusion. One of the clearest was constructed by the genius of Dostoevski in that section of his novel, *The Brothers Karamazov*, in which the central figure is the Grand Inquisitor. The setting is in Spain at the time when Europe was writhing under the Inquisition. The purpose of the Inquisition was good; namely, to protect the Church from heresy. But as bigoted minds and cruel spirits got possession of the machinery of the Inquisition, it became the destroyer of heresy and heretics alike; it became the noose that sought to strangle the freedoms of Europe in every area of life. Devoted to the Church, the Inquisition would admit no change or criticism within the Church. It insisted upon the sanctity of the Church and demanded unqualified conformity to her edicts. One of the men haled before the Grand Inquisitor as a dangerous influence to the Church was Jesus Christ himself who had returned to earth to see how the faith he planted was faring. What a conversation ensues, as visualized by the novelist! We need to read it again and again—especially when we get complacent about our church and critical of any and every move to change it! The irony of one concept of churchmanship comes to its perfect climax when the Grand Inquisitor orders the execution of Jesus as an enemy of the true Faith as found in the Christian Church!

That, surely, is the appetite of iniquity let loose in the Church— and it can get loose in every church! When the Church becomes an end in herself rather than being a humble servant of the Word of God—watch out! When she throws up ramparts around creedal, ecclesiastical and liturgical forms—be on your guard! When she is so intent upon saving her life that she forgets to lose it—crucifixions are on their way! When she refuses to exalt the Kingdom of God above the kingdoms of this world and is fearful about bringing the kingdoms of this earth under the judgment of the Kingdom of God—she may be many things, but she is no longer the Church of God. Iniquity hath eaten her up; she is wholly consumed. Though men may praise her as "doing her duty," as being "the bulwalk of our way of life"—the angels round about God's throne weep bitter tears because Calvary was for nought and the tragedy of the Crucifixion must be enacted again.

Who of us seeing this happen—feeling it happen deep within us—can help echoing Satan's wretched cry, "Myself am hell!"

Indulgence in iniquity in any form is the most dangerous practice anyone can get into—whether a person or an institution. The only safeguard against it is to learn how to live humbly and in a spirit of complete commitment to the will of the good God who is above all and in all. Our good is never good enough; our virtue is never virtuous enough; our piety is never pure enough to enable us to be other than humbly prostrate before the God of all. To know this, to accept it, to be guided by it day by day throughout our life is to give our answer to an ancient question, "What doth the Lord require of thee but to deal justly, to love mercy, and to walk humbly with thy God?"

IV

Pick the Right Ancestors[1]

SCRIPTURE LESSON: Psalm 16

TEXT: The lines are fallen unto me in pleasant places;
Yea, I have a goodly heritage.

I

IN A WORLD where tradition has lost much of its force, where custom and convention no longer persuade and coerce as once they did, we are in danger of misunderstanding their role in life. In our pursuit of freedom we have turned away from tradition, little realizing that it is an essential aspect of a stable, creative life and society. We once thought freedom consisted in throwing off all claims of tradition and all coercion born of custom and convention. We not only thought it, we tried to live it. And, on the basis of our experience, we are able to say with some definiteness that whoever tries it will wind up a sadder, wiser people. The great problem posed by convention and custom is not how to get rid of them, but how to live with them in such fashion as not to be stifled by them; how to manage them rather than be managed by them; how to be strengthened and freed by them rather than enfeebled and finally enslaved by them.

While this particular problem emerges in every area of life, we are feeling it with a special urgency today as we celebrate the independence of our country. I suggest as an excellent approach to it a verse from the 16th Psalm:

[1] Preached on Independence Sunday.

The lines are fallen unto me in pleasant places;
Yea, I have a goodly heritage.

These words, wrung as they were out of the Psalmist's own experience as well as that of his people, will, I believe, throw some light
on our problem today. For if ever a people needed to recover the
confidence that makes these words of the Psalmist radiant, we are
that people. We have a heritage, but is it a goodly one? Responsibility has fallen to us with a vengeance, but is it a pleasant responsibility? And I suggest that this season of the year when we
celebrate our birth as a nation is a proper time in which to investigate these questions.

While we cannot be sure of the exact circumstances that surrounded the Psalmist as he wrote his expression of faith in his heritage, we know enough about the general situation to fill in most of
the background. He belonged to a tiny nation that had served as
the football for the more powerful nations to the northeast and the
south. Israel had known few periods of peace and none free from
the threat or the actual fact of war itself. She had seen her great
cities destroyed, her leaders taken captive, her temples desecrated
and destroyed. She had seen a remnant of survivors come back
from exile and start all over again, rebuilding the city, the temple,
and the spiritual and moral fabric of the people.

Looking back on all this—an experience that stretched over several hundred years—the Psalmist lifts his voice in praise to the God
of his fathers. He sees in all that has happened to his people, the
hand of God dealing with his people. He says with almost discon-
certing quietness and conviction, "I have a goodly heritage." We
must not misunderstand him to say, "My heritage is all good."
That would have been untrue. There was much of evil in this
inheritance; its landscape was dotted with some of the most colos-
sal and humiliating follies known to man, and the Psalmist could
see that at least as plainly as we do—and maybe more so.

In saying that he had a goodly heritage, the Psalmist was rejoic-
·ing in the evidence of the goodness of God in the life of his
people; he was gratefully acknowledging the existence of men like
Abraham, Joseph, Moses, and others whose great faith and courage

had led Israel over many a hazardous mile. He was seeing again the prophets of preceding centuries who were raised up of God to bring his people under judgment and to put their feet on the right paths again. He was rejoicing in the determination and courage of men like Nehemiah and Ezra who could rebuild the shattered morale as well as the cities and the temple of Israel after the return from the Exile. Looking on these clear evidences of the hand of God in the life of His people, the Psalmist is not afraid to take up the lines of responsibility that fall to him and his generation. For the God who has brought them thus far will continue to be with them—if they will but worship and seek to serve Him; this is the faith of the Psalmist.

It appears to me that the Psalmist did an excellent job of an extremely difficult task: *selecting the right ancestors.* And having selected them for good and sufficient reason, he both rejoices in them and deliberately assumes the responsibility of associating with them in his own time.

The Psalmist is not alone in his effort to select the right ancestors from his religious tradition. The opening utterance of Jesus' public career was, in effect, a selecting of ancestors. You recall how he went to the synagogue on the Sabbath day, opened the book of Isaiah, read the passage which outlined the work of the Messiah, and said, "This day is this Scripture fulfilled in your ears." He might as well have said, "This is where I stand in our religious tradition." To a people who made much of ancestral tradition, this announcement was a shock. Yet they knew exactly what he was planning to be and to do. Needless to say they were astounded. They thought they had known this young man—and they had! They had known him as neighbor, friend, artisan, and perhaps as wise counselor in the affairs of their common life. But when he indicated the spiritual ancestors he was picking, they saw him with new eyes. For they realized, as we do now, that a man is known by the ancestors he picks. From that memorable occasion to our own there has been an indissoluble connection between the prophets of ancient Israel whom Jesus selected as his ancestors at that time, and the Christian faith. Jesus not only picked his own ancestors upon this occasion, he picked at least some of the ancestors of all who were to follow after him in the Christian tradition.

Still another example of picking ancestors is to be found in the eleventh chapter of the book of Hebrews in the New Testament. The writer is building up an imposing list of heroes of the faith: of the people who deserve to be exalted in the thought and life of Christians who try to live by faith. Beginning with Abraham he says of them all, "By faith . . ." they did this and this and this. Guided by this formula, the writer strode through the entire history of the Hebrew people down to his own time and as we study the places where he put down his feet over that thirteen-hundred-year period, we discover that we are in a choice collection of spiritual giants. That, of course, was the intention of the writer of the book. He, like the Psalmist and Jesus before him, was doing a remarkably effective job of picking the right ancestors.

II

Most of us have heard the advice of a geneticist that the first step toward a good life is to select the right kind of ancestors. The geneticist, true to his trade, was matching genes and chromosomes and may have been toying with the idea of a selective breeding up of the quality of the human strain—much as the animal breeder builds up a blood strain in his stock. He is referring to one kind of ancestry—biological ancestry—the kind about which we have no option so far as our ancestors are concerned. How much and in what ways and by what means they determine what we are is good for many a long session among biologists before they get it settled —if ever. But it is clear that we have no power of selection in this part of our inheritance. It is what it is—and must be accepted as such.

But there are other ancestors, among whom we, like the Psalmist and his spiritual colleagues, can pick and choose—among whom we must pick and choose. For you can tell a man or a church or a people by the kind of ancestors they select.

Plato would be glad to lend the powerful support of his great mind to this ancient insight. He knew and feared the power of the poet in his Republic because they could corrupt the youth of his country with their glamorous tales of unworthy heroes. Plato did not object to poets as such, but he wanted them to do a certain piece of work in the perfect state. He knew he needed them to exalt men who properly were heroes and deserved emulation by the youth of Athens, but he did not trust the poets to select the right ancestors. Like every other writer on such themes, he wanted to do that himself and do it for everyone else!

Entirely apart from the justice or even the wisdom of Plato's evaluation of their ability to pick the right kind of heroes, who can doubt his realism in dealing with the poets even before he turns to the teachers and the lawmakers of his Republic? He knew the truth of a judgment made by Andrew Fletcher many years ago, "Give me the making of the songs of a nation, and I care not who makes its laws." The mythology cherished by a people, the heroic tales of gods and men, the legends and traditions which became the stuff of history—all these will tell you at least as much about them as the laws they enact. In fact, in point of time, they will tell you more because they will account for the general tenor or moral tone of the laws themselves. Any thorough study of the life and history of a people ought to begin in this nebulous area of their dreams, songs, legends and myths.

When Mussolini began chanting about reviving the glories of the Caesars, when Hitler and Rosenberg picked Thor and other war gods from the obscurity of Nordic mythology and began to parade them before the German people, especially the youth, thoughtful people knew that trouble was ahead. They had selected the wrong ancestors for praise and emulation. Somewhere in the traditions of every people are many such ancestors whose just fate is to be forgotten by their children. Yet when their children, whether through fear or pride or greed, select and resurrect them, they not only become symbols of their ancestors at their worst, but they actually provide a kind of moral backing for their children as they proceed to cry and make havoc throughout life. It is of utmost practical concern, then, to pick the right ancestors since by so doing we are rejecting the wrong ones.

Those of us who want to be Christian churchmen as well as Christian citizens in this land that we love need to take this lesson seriously to heart.

III

Like the Psalmist, I feel that we have a goodly heritage in this land of ours. Not a heritage that is all and evenly good, but one that has great good in it. And I know I speak in a representative rather than a personal capacity when I say that. Most of us do have a goodly heritage providing we feel free to be honest about it.

This is certainly true of our family tradition. Fortunately for us, there are not many Jukes families in existence! Most of us come from a line of people who, on the whole, have given us a basic health of body, mind and spirit—and, for this we need to be everlastingly grateful. Even when physical frailties seem to be inherited, they are usually accompanied by the example of how they can be wisely managed. Lest you think I am going to lead you in a collective prostration at the foot of that god, The Family Tree, let me emphasize the fact that our ancestors are what my father used to call "a mixed breed." Some are good, some not; some energetic, some slothful in the extreme; some dependable, some not; some a joy to their homes and families, some decidedly not. I do not know of any family tree that is as uniformly sound in all its branches as some of its later sprouts wish it were and pretend it is.

A close friend of mine in Iowa was working up his family tree a few years ago and having a great time doing it. He had good reason to be proud of the remarkable line of men of integrity and high community repute that emerged from the family as it moved from Boston to Iowa over the course of a hundred years. While on a trip to Vermont a few years after he started working out the family tree, he decided to look up the grave of one of his forebears about whom little was known. You can guess the rest: He found him in the section of an old cemetery reserved for bums and paupers! Needless to say, I've had greater confidence in my friend's report of the rest of his ancestors since he began including this one as well!

One of the elemental and fundamental duties of parenthood is to teach children an honest and selective appreciation of the family tradition. Only thus can we overcome the rootless feeling which plagues our generation. A child feels that he belongs to something that includes but far transcends the immediate family. It is about time we took the family album out of the category of Mid-Victorian stuffiness and recognized its enormous influence in making our family traditions come alive. Some of the most interesting moments in my childhood center in such an album and in the stories my parents were fond of telling over and over again about the characters there (some deserving the title of "character" on all counts!). One of the truly stabilizing factors in the growth of a child in this too-hurried, too-fearful, too-irritable, too-scattered civilization of ours is to renew with frequency his sense of kinship with his family tradition.

Edmund Burke was speaking a rock-bottom truth when he said, "People will never look forward to posterity who never look backward to their ancestors." Quite obviously, this task is going to be done at home or not at all. Parents, grandparents, and all other relatives are needed for the work.

Looking back on this family tradition, you and I can say with the Psalmist, "The lines are fallen unto me in pleasant places. Yea, I have a goodly heritage."

IV

We Americans live in the midst of one of the greatest paradoxes in history, a paradox which can be described a number of ways:

1. The most powerful nation on earth is more than half hysterical with fear. She is led as much by fancy as by fact. She is not only justly concerned about friend and enemy, she is unjustly critical and suspicious of both.

2. The nation that has done more than any other to light the flame of hope in the human heart is almost numb with despair herself. Once willing to take a chance on almost anyone who wanted to make a new life in America—an experiment which has abundantly proved its worth—she

now hems and haws over the admission of a small number of displaced persons who want to come to this country and in the revision of the Immigration Act practically shuts off immigration.

3. The people who have wanted peace above almost all else are now arming at a rate and in a mood that not only warns their enemies but worries their friends—a fact driven home to me over and over again in my visit to Latin America in 1951.

4. The people whose ingenuity and courage have vanquished problem after problem seem now to have lost faith in their ability to do much more than multiply weapons of war. Yet even as they multiply weapons of war their faith in their ability to use them wisely and well progressively diminishes and threatens finally to disappear.

5. The people who have had the patience, the will and the energy to settle and develop a vast continent in the brief span of three hundred years seem utterly unable to bring these virtues to bear in any effective way upon the new problems they must face today. They seem to be on the point of forsaking what James Truslow Adams has called "The American Dream" for a nightmarish existence within the ever-heightening walls of power, fear and suspicion.

As a net result of all this our entire civilization is obviously in a time of troubles and we instead of being a stabilizing factor may well be one of the sources of greatest uncertainty. This fact shouts at us from Korea, Indo-China, Europe and South America as well as from our own common life. No one can pretend that he knows a sure way out of this agony, but a certain first step is to recover some confidence in our tradition, our ancestry, our dream, our experience, our abilities, and the fundamental institutions of our country. Actually what we need now above all else is a good dose of the idealism and realism which have combined to make this country what she is today. We need to make the wisest kind of selection among our many ancestors, rejecting the ones who would aggravate our problems, and accepting those who would help us on our and their journey.

V.

As we go about this important task of picking the right ancestors, I suggest that we ought to search for certain qualities rather than for certain men. Which means that while no one man will be a perfect embodiment of any given quality we seek, it will be one of the great facts about him. Even as we may deplore his deficiencies—and, since he is human, he will have many—and as we chuckle over his peculiarities—and even famous men have some—we will nonetheless think him worthy of being held before us and our children as a great man, one worthy of respect and emulation because of his devotion to this quality.

I suggest that we pick as our ancestors men who were passionately devoted to freedom under God. I think again of the Pilgrims whose freedom was a trust from God—a trust of which they were stewards. We need as ancestors men who wanted this kind of freedom not only for themselves but for others as well; men who not only had the will to say "freedom under God" but also the courage to seek it for themselves and the even greater courage to share it with others. And I do not want as picked ancestors, men who are afraid of freedom or who are selfish about it. God knows we do not need men like that to encourage us in many of the travesties now being perpetrated in the name of freedom. We need to have the same kind of faith in freedom that we profess to have in truth, in God.

How fortunate we are to have had not one, nor a few, but many ancestors whose love of freedom under God was the consuming passion of their lives! And how we need them, and need to own them, today! Thanks to them, freedom and America are inseparable. If you love America, you will love freedom. When you doubt or lose faith in freedom, you are doubting and losing faith in America. When you seek to curtail freedom, you strike at the heart of the genius of this land. When you openly or covertly deny the fact and practice of freedom, you betray America.

It is not an easy thing, as well we know, to try to incorporate the meaning of freedom in the conventions, laws, industries and institutions of a great and growing country. Problems aplenty abound on every side as we continue in this task. But, as I have faith in freedom and America, I know we can work these problems out one by one. In this season when we celebrate independence I propose to exalt the kind of ancestors who can help us at our task today, and I should like to be known to my children as one who was glad to stand in the tradition of freedom-loving, freedom-believing, freedom-serving men and women.

I should like to suggest that we have some ancestors who fill this bill: the Pilgrims, the Puritans, and every other religiously-minded group that left their homelands and came to this country. They were not plaster saints, deserving of even low pedestals, but they do belong in the eleventh chapter of Hebrews, among those who "by faith" went out not knowing what lay ahead but knowing that they went forth in the providence of God. On this, as on a firm foundation, they rested their ethical and moral code, their ideas of right and wrong, good and evil, truth and falsehood. I do not mean that they were always guided by those codes—that, obviously, is not true—but I do mean that they never once doubted the reality of the moral foundations of life. Our need for recapturing this spiritual heritage is too great to require argument these days.

In the 1920's the late Dean Inge, known as the "Gloomy Dean," passed a sober judgment on his beloved England. Speaking to his fellow countrymen, he warned them that one of "our greatest weaknesses is our neglect of the magnificent spiritual heritage which we possess in our history and literature." If we may believe the reports of the lack of direct and conscious concern on the part of the British people now about their spiritual heritage, the Dean's warning was wasted. Unless some way can be found to arrest the decline in interest in churches and the Christian conception of life, his worst fears will be realized. Nor is England alone in this plight.

An almost identical judgment was passed on our beloved country by one of our religious leaders at about the same time Dean Inge was speaking to England, "America is today running on the momentum of a godly ancestry. When that momentum runs down, God help America." There is something almost pathetic about Gamaliel Bradford's letter to a friend,

I have long been convinced that the greatest need of American civilization today is the need of God. . . . Personally, I am in no position to make any effort in the matter, but because, while I feel that the whole universe crumbles without God, I am myself utterly unable to find Him. I am only deploring what I am sure is an imperative need, without being able to suggest any means of meeting it. I trust someone, with a more positive faith, will be able to do better.

There is one thing I am sure we can do about it—something Gamaliel Bradford and his friends could do too if they would— and that is to pick the right kind of ancestors for elevation and emulation in our common life. They will set a tone, give a direction to thought and life that may well prove to be decisive.

When we say with the Psalmist, "Yea, I have a goodly heritage," let us add to faith in freedom under God a second quality that we seek in these ancestors we pick—tolerance: tolerance of differences in race and religion, in political, social and economic views; tolerance of criticism, whether responsible or irresponsible in origin and nature; tolerance of minority groups and movements that frequently get on fire and in their zeal threaten to ignite our social order.

Arbitration, negotiation, conciliation—these are the true methods of tolerance in the face of differences. Yet, today, they are treated as synonyms for lack of conviction, weak will and appeasement. We have the attitude attributed to Hermann Goering when before World War II he said that the Nazis were determined to have their way or to wreck Europe. As I hear and read speeches on many controversial subjects today, I hear ominous overtones of the same destructive intolerance. When I recall the appalling differences that existed in early America about the nature and the powers of the new government, the proper foreign policy for it, the relationship between federal and state governments and a dozen other matters, I marvel at the amount of tolerance there must have been in our leadership then in order to get together at all and to stay together long enough to reach working agreements. But they did it—and so should we. There is something downright disgraceful about the bitterness and intolerance that are coming to be the accepted characteristic of public discussion on controversial matters. I am not pleading for soft-pedaling any issue or any facts about any issue, but I am saying that we need to feel the responsibility of approaching these issues in a far different spirit than most of us now do or see done. And the key to that necessary difference is found in the word "tolerance."

One of the best parts of our goodly heritage, and one that we need to emphasize as we pick our ancestors, is *faith in the future:* faith in our way of life; faith in the creative, dynamic, dependable nature of the great ideals that are a part of our heritage.

It could not have been easy for Washington, Jefferson, Franklin and their colleagues consciously and knowingly to turn their backs on many precious ancestral ways and ideas and forge ahead into the unknown future of this new land. But they did it because they shared with Columbus the vision attributed to him by Santayana: [2]

> Columbus found a world, and had no chart,
> Save one that faith deciphered in the skies;
> To trust the soul's invincible surmise
> Was all his science and his only art.
> Our knowledge is a torch of smoky pine
> That lights the pathway but one step ahead
> Across a void of mystery and dread.
> Bid, then, the tender light of faith to shine
> By which alone the mortal heart is led
> Unto the thinking of the thought divine.

Facing as we surely do another "void of mystery and dread" over which we must somehow find and build a way, we need to have not "the tender light" but the powerful light of a great faith in our heritage, our ideals, in each other, and in the God who will provide

[2] "O World," from *Poems* by George Santayana. Copyright, 1923, by Charles Scribner's Sons, 1951, by George Santayana. Reprinted by permission of the publisher.

the light and leading we need. We can have it if we have the humility and the patience to seek it, and if, when found in some measure, we have the courage to implement it in our lives.

That this attitude toward past, present and future both seeks and welcomes changes in our traditional ways of thinking and living must be obvious to all. Changes have come in the past—not once but many times, not superficial changes but deep-lying ones —and after a period of adjustment they have become an accepted part of our way of life. No one can arrest this dynamic unfoldment of our society, our country and our world—nor should we want to even if we could. But we must share in it not blindly but keenly aware of what we are doing, bringing every ounce of experience, criticism and judgment to bear upon proposed changes but never once doubting that changes must come.

In doing this, we do not desert our ancestors even as we break with their own ways of thought and life. We do but follow their own example relative to their ancestors. We know even as they knew that "no generation can merely reproduce its ancestors"—it must accept its goodly heritage and, under the guidance of God, seek to improve upon it. Let us then, in this spirit, enter into the celebration of Independence Week in our common life here in America.

V

When I Am With God

I

WHEN a distinguished psychiatrist referred to us as a "neurotic age," the facts were all on his side. The rapid and, as yet, unchecked increase in ailments due to emotional disturbance and tension is one of the acknowledged scandals of modern civilization as well as one of the greatest perplexities of medical science. The boast frequently heard half a century ago that the increase in leisure-time activities and vacation periods would make us a happier, healthier people has been silenced by grim facts. We may live longer than we used to, but it is yet to be proved that our longer lives are happier, more useful, more satisfying, more creative than the shorter ones of our fathers. We are a nervous, taut, hard-pressed, harried, easily upset, easily irritated and easily exhausted generation. We have not learned how to avoid unwholesome tensions; we have not learned how to manage or reduce them once we get them—or they get us. And they distort our view, our energies, and usually paralyze thought and action with fear at precisely the times when they are needed most.

Facts like these prompted the physician, Alexis Carrell, to observe that man simply does not have the nervous equipment to keep pace with modern civilization.

Not all physicians give us up as hopeless, though. A number of years ago a prominent doctor advised us to regard the management of tensions as one of the major health problems of our time. He said that there were three things to do about it.

49

First, "look inside yourself"—understand the glandular meaning of fear, anger, worry and hate; realize that these emotions actually upset the balance of the entire system in so radical a fashion that they can and will lead to nervous breakdown if indulged in too frequently. Second, "look at yourself" says the doctor. He documents this in a remorseless way: "If we who rush and worry needlessly could see ourselves as others see us, simple pride would stop us. Let a morbidly distraught woman consult her mirror when she is under the lash of our [emotional] tyrants; her face ugly with frowns, her jaws clinched. Cosmetic tricks won't banish these beauty destroyers." Third, look away from yourself. Practice lifting your mind, every now and again, above the rush and confusion around you. Take time out during your busiest day to think of something pleasant." [1]

I am quite willing to let the physicians look inside us and the beauty experts look at us, but there is something religious faith wants to say about the third—looking away from ourselves. This suggests one answer to the question of the place of devotion in life. The value of this look away from ourselves will depend entirely upon what we look at. The doctor suggests we look at something pleasant. So far, so good, I suppose, but surely we can do better than that! At least historic religion thinks so. It advises us to look away from ourselves by looking toward God.

"I will lift up mine eyes unto the hills. Whence cometh my help? My help cometh from the Lord who made heaven and earth"—is one way of putting it. Another is the 19th Psalm—read earlier in the service—which bids us look away from ourselves not that we may simply enjoy something or other but that we may contemplate and stand in awe of the glory of God, the Creator of all, and rejoice in His care for and mercy toward us. Never has the religious look away from oneself been put in more personal and sensitive terms than these: "Let the words of my mouth and the meditation of my heart be acceptable in thy sight, O Lord, my rock and my redeemer."

Here is the very heart of religious devotion: An awareness of

[1] Richard H. Hoffman, M.D., in *Reader's Digest*, August, 1951, pp. 143–44.

God, an awareness of one's dependence upon Him, a sincere acceptance of that relationship. Here is a man—a person like any one of us—honestly and humbly looking away from himself, looking toward God, then in the strength of that, coming back for another look at himself.

II

Once we see what devotion is, what it means, we will make a place for it in our daily life—of that I have no doubt.

Devotion, in a word, is the conscious, habitual effort to look toward God. It is that period in our day when we try to center our thoughts on God, when, through meditation and prayer, we approach Him in a deeply personal way.

The nun reading her prayers as she hurtles toward the loop on the El is engaged in devotion. The man who at a stated time each day reads his Bible and repeats a prayer is engaged in devotions. The person who comes into a chapel for meditation and prayer is engaged in devotions. I have never found a better interpretation of what devotion means to one who practices it than Walter Rauschenbusch's poem, "The Postern Gate":

> In the castle of my soul
> Is a little postern gate,
> Whereat, when I enter,
> I am in the presence of God.
> In a moment, in the turning of a thought,
> I am where God is.
> This is a fact.

And then the poet suggests several meanings of this great fact:

> This world of ours has length and breadth,
> A superficial and horizontal world.
> When I am with God
> I look deep down and high up,
> And all is changed.[2]

How changed? For one thing, we sense anew the mystery of life,

[2] From D. R. Sharpe, *Walter Rauschenbusch*, Copyright, 1942, by The Macmillan Company. Reprinted by permission of the publisher.

the vastness of the universe, the glory of our privilege of sharing in it. Most of us get so busy with programs and plans and schedules and techniques that we forget the ancient affirmation, "Be still, and know that I am God!" We are so preoccupied with our problems, worries, fears and hates that we forget to "worship the Lord in the beauty of holiness"—or in any other way at all, for that matter. We forget to worship, period. And when we do, life gets wholly out of perspective.

The late H. G. Wells was one of the most gifted men of his generation: brilliant mind, tireless student, keen prophet and an excellent writer. But there was a puzzling despair and doubt hovering over all that he wrote. The longer he lived the gloomier he became until, in his last public interview, he gave up the cause of civilization as hopeless. Wells gives us the clue to his morbid outlook in this autobiographical note, "There was a time when my little soul shone and was uplifted at the starry enigma of the sky. That has gone absolutely. Now I can go out and look at the stars as I look at the pattern of wallpaper on a railway station waiting room."

What a falling off that is from the Psalmist's awed cry, "The heavens are telling the glory of God; and the firmament proclaims his handiwork." John Ruskin was right when he hurled this challenge at a generation that thought the meaning of life could be found in the accumulation of wealth, "I would sooner live in a cottage and wonder at everything, than live in Warwick Castle and wonder at nothing."

How long will it take us to learn that when we begin to lose our sense of the mystery of life we shall soon be losing our grip on the meaning of life? And when that happens a good deal of adolescent and half-hysterical bragging is certain to take place about the glory of man. We begin to chant with Swinburne,

> Glory to man in the highest
> For man is the master of things.

And we wind up dropping atomic bombs all over the world.

One can be proud of the progress man has made, can rejoice in

his many rich achievements, and still know that the glory of man
is a poor substitute for the glory of God. And no one has known
this more truly or stated it more fearlessly than the men whom we
gladly acknowledge to be our greatest. They, at least, have no intention of posing as God! "Why callest thou me good?" the greatest of all demanded; "There is none good but one, even God!"

Lose that sense of the mystery of life surrounding us personally
and overarching the generations, and we will have lost more than
a desire to worship God; we will soon lose our reason for hope and
faith in man, including ourselves.

> When I am with God
> I look deep down and high up
> And all is changed.

III

The poet suggests another value of devotion—one we have been
anticipating in what we have just been saying,

> When I am with God
> All life has a meaning.

It is God's meaning for life that we always seek and sometimes
find in our devotions. There is no way of estimating the difference
this discovery makes in a number of very concrete ways. It gives
us a new answer to the question, "Who am I?"

One of the most poignant lines in *The Death of a Salesman* is
Willie Loman's insistence, "I have a right to know who I am." Of
course he does. So does every man. One of the marks of maturity
is the exercise of this right in a thoroughly responsible fashion. But
how did Willie Loman try to discover who he was? By looking
inside himself, at himself, and never away from himself and never,
never, toward God. He was looking for the right thing in the wrong
place and in the wrong way. Is it any wonder that he found nothing worth living for, that despair and defeat are the final movements in his spiritual—or should we say "spiritless"—pilgrimage?

Religion has a conviction, one born of and bolstered by thousands of years of human experience, that life has real meaning,

God's meaning; that the Willie Lomans of this world, asking after it, can find it at least in part; and that in the finding of it we can discover who we are.

As we look away from ourselves, looking toward God in a spirit of devotion, we discover several important facts about life. We discover God as the Creator of all, the One in whom "we live and move and have our being," "Our Father." This is the true setting of life, and we must see ourselves in it if we would discover the real meaning of our life. The glory of religious faith is the way it sets everyone and everything against this backdrop of eternity. Sincere devotion guides us to the knowledge that we are the children of God; it never permits us to think that we are god. We begin then with the simple assurance that the most important thing about us, and it ought to be the most important thing to us, is God's purpose in creating us. Once see ourselves as the children of God, and we cannot escape the conviction that we ought so to regard all other men and ought to judge our relationships with them by that fact.

> When I am with God
> All life has a meaning—

A meaning in which

> Big things become small, and small things
> become great.
> The near becomes far, and the future is
> near.
> The lowly and despised is shot through
> with glory.

What fairer fruit of devotion could one seek than this: A vision of the true worth of what we do day by day? Every preacher needs it, I know. And I am sure every businessman, every parent, and every student needs it too. It is appallingly easy to get all mixed up about the relative worth of what we do. When that happens, chaos moves in. We find ourselves measuring the worth of our lives by the number of organizations we belong to rather than by the quality of what we contribute to them and through them. Mothers bemoan the time their families take, thinking they would rather spend it at the bridge table or on the golf links, or even in church organizations. Husbands and wives count a quiet evening at home as "lost" and wish for a continuous whirl of activities outside the house. Students feel that they are missing out on a lot if they concentrate on their studies and give little time to the blinding whirl of campus life.

If we are not aware of this danger and on guard against it, we will become "hollow men," empty of conviction, empty of purpose, and empty of any sense of real value at all.

I cannot say that the habit of daily devotion is a guarantee that this will not happen, but I can say that it is the best guarantee we have. It reminds me of a small boy's description of what salt is: "Salt is what spoils the potatoes when you leave it out." Devotion is what spoils life when we leave it out. When we put it in and put it in regularly we have our best chance to keep our values in order, our lives in proportion, and our vision of life's meaning bright and beautiful.

IV

The poet assures us, further, that devotion is as deeply social as it is intensely personal:

> When I am with God
> My fellow men are not far-off and forgotten,
> But close and strangely dear . . .
> They shine, as if a light were glowing within them
> Even those who frown on me
> And love me not
> Seem part of the great scheme of God. . . .

Devotion, then, is more than the effort of man to rediscover God and himself; it results, consciously or not, in the rediscovery of the true brotherhood of all men.

Most of us believe in the brotherhood of man but in a limited sort of way. That is, we want to pick the brothers who are to be admitted. And when the picking is over we have admitted those who think as we do, believe as we do, perhaps even pray and look as we do.

The brotherhood of man that great religion talks about is a quite different thing. It actually includes all men, no matter who they are or what they have done. The brotherhood of man that we discover in devotion is of this sort. It includes all—even our enemies. Until one has made that discovery for himself through religious experience it is hard to get him to see that it is not only possible but inescapable. Yet it is possible to feel a deep sense of oneness with, understanding of and sympathy with, those who on the surface appear to be our enemies. Most of us hesitate over it though, feeling a little like the son who was exasperated by his wonderful mother's determination to see good in even bad people. "Mother," he exclaimed, "I think you could see good in the devil himself." To which she replied instantly and gravely, "Well, he is persistent."

If we are fond of our fears, our hates and our prejudices, let us stay away from the practice of looking toward God, for in the long run, it will undermine them all by digging down to the firm foundation of the brotherhood of all men—and once there, it will demand that we build a life and a society worthy of the foundation.

V

Let those who have engaged in it speak about the cleansing and strengthening of mind and spirit that come through the practice of devotion.

> When I am with God
> My fear is gone
> In the great quiet of God.
> My troubles are as the pebbles on the road,
> My joys are like the everlasting hills.

Judge Harold R. Medina who presided at the trial of the eleven Communist leaders in New York in 1949 made an address before a group of churchmen some months later. He told how the tension and torment of that sensational case had worn him to the breaking point. Finally, he said,

I had to leave the court room and lie down in my chambers. Let me be frank: I was thinking then that perhaps I should never go back. In my weakness it seemed to me at last that I had stood as much as I could for as long as I could. I could not endure more of it. I was ready to give up.

But, instead, like a frightened child calling to his father in the dark, I asked God to take charge of things and that His will be done. I cannot report any mysterious or supernatural experience as a result of that prayer. All I know is that, as I lay on the couch in the heat of that darkened chamber, some kind of new strength seemed to flow into my veins. That brief period of communion with my Maker saved my life and saved the trial. After 15 minutes I was refreshed, and went back to carry on the business of my court.

And I gained in strength from that moment on to the end. For Someone else was with me, all the way.[3]

Looking toward God can give us at least a portion of peace with the work of each day that seems to have been felt by John Wesley and St. Francis of Assisi. Both were asked essentially the same question and made essentially the same answer.

When John Wesley was asked by a lady how he would spend his time if he knew he would die at twelve o'clock the next day at midnight, he answered, "Why, just as I had expected to spend the time. I would preach at Gloucester tonight and tomorrow morning, at Tewkesbury in the afternoon, go to my friend Martin's house for entertainment, converse and pray with the family as usual, retire to my room at ten o'clock, commend myself to my heavenly Father, lie down to rest, and wake up in glory."

St. Francis was hoeing in his garden when the question was put to him by an ardent follower as to what he would do if he were suddenly to learn that he were to die at sunset that very day. He replied, "I would finish hoeing my garden."

When I am with God, life takes on new meaning—this is the unqualified testimony of those who in the fine old phrase have "practiced the presence of God" daily. I can think of many great gifts parents might give their children, but I can think of no

[3] *Reader's Digest*, August, 1951, p. 18.

greater gift than this: That by their habit, by their example and by their admonition their children shall learn the meaning, the worth, the strength of devotion; that something of the power, the direction and the poise that can come only through this practice of the presence of God will be a part of their daily life.

Yet there is a sense in which it is misleading to say, "When I am with God." Strictly, we are with Him all of the time. We cannot get away from Him. This is His universe, His world, His life that we live—not ours. He surrounds us as the sunlight surrounds the houses in which we live. Yet we live in darkness. We have let care, worry, fear and hatred pull down the blinds of our minds and seal the doors of our lives until we seem to be lost, alone, forsaken. But it is a lostness, an aloneness, a forsakenness of our own making, not of God's. For He wants to enter in and have communion with us—but we must open the door.

> Grant us such grace that we may work thy will
> And speak thy word and walk before thy face,
> Profound and calm, like waters deep and still;
> Grant us such grace.[4]

[4] Christina Georgina Rossetti.

VI

Life Demands Loyalties

~~~~~~

SCRIPTURE LESSON: Psalm 27:1–14

I

THE word "loyalty" has been keeping such questionable company of late that one cannot help wondering whether it is not now itself deeply corrupted. Evil communications, we have been told, corrupt good manners, and, we may be sure, evil companions corrupt good morals. That is why we have a right to be concerned about the good name of "loyalty." Fanaticism of every kind, bigotry of every shade, racism, nationalism and sectarianism—all these have presented and now present themselves as examples of loyalty. We meet the demand for loyalty oaths everywhere. Loyalty oaths, so conceived and insisted upon, are a far cry from being an opportunity to bear glad witness to one's faith in this country. In actual intention and use they are advanced as the legal basis for possible charges of perjury, and, what is worse, they are advanced in the spirit of the rack and screw—those infamous instruments of torture of the Inquisition.

Actually we have talked and scared ourselves into quite a state of mind and society on this matter of loyalty. We simply do not have anything like the same amount of freedom for discussion and criticism and redirection of our way of life and the institutions of our land that was enjoyed by Washington, Jefferson, Franklin and Hamilton. Let a man come up with a fundamental criticism of our way of life, and he is immediately awarded a pink or red label. Let a church, this church, The Methodist Church, or the World

59

Council of Churches insist upon and engage in the right to bring our life and times under the judgment of the will of God as we see it in Jesus Christ, and, with fine disregard for every known fact of Christian thought and history, some will label us "fellow travelers." Men who do this sort of thing deserve the same kind of sympathetic, yet objective, hearing that a psychiatrist gives a patient whose neurosis roots in fear. They are not to be scorned or hated; they are not even to be pitied; they are to be understood and dealt with patiently and gently for the sick people they are.

But despite the many crimes committed in the name of loyalty we cannot escape it. Nor would we if we could. Life is literally unthinkable and would truly be unlivable without the many loyalties that give meaning and character to it.

Look for a moment at the essential meaning of loyalty and we will be in a position to do a number of things: (1) to appreciate its importance to life; (2) to recognize the great dangers implicit in it; (3) to see the profound relationship between great religion and great loyalties.

When we say we are loyal to an idea like democracy, or a cause like Christianity, or an institution like the Church, what, essentially, do we mean? We mean that, to some extent at least, we understand it, that we believe in it and in the importance of what it stands for, that we are willing to be identified with it and will work with and for it.

When we say we are loyal to a person, we mean that we know him, that we have confidence in him as a person, that we are not only glad to be known as his friend but that we insist upon so being known, that we propose to stand by him through thick and thin; that, in short, he has a claim upon us—a claim that we both freely acknowledge and seek to honor with our life.

When we say we want to be loyal to God we mean, in all humility, that we know Him in the intimate sense of having had experiences of His presence and meaning in life, that we believe in Him as Creator, Sustainer, Redeemer of the world, that we propose to let this faith be the distinctive thing about our personal life as well as our relationships.

Loyalty, so conceived, is more, much more, than an interest in someone or something. It is a personal commitment to someone or something. The final movement in loyalty is always this: *Here I am. You can count on me!* Loyalty is a positive rather than a negative attitude. When it is wholesome and creative it is born of faith not fear; of knowledge not ignorance; of awareness not blindness. But when fear, ignorance and blindness determine our loyalties, as indeed they can, then loyalty becomes an evil, not a creative force in human life.

Thus the dual problem before us seems to be this: How to find the kind of loyalty that is creative; how to keep it from being corrupted by our fears, our blindness and our ignorance.

II

We need loyalty in life—there can be no mistake about that. It is a requirement not an elective in this business of living. Let anyone try to get along without it and he will feel the full truth of W. B. Yeats's sober description of the modern world:

> Things fall apart; the center cannot hold;
> Mere anarchy is loosed upon the world;
> The best lack all conviction, while the worst
> Are full of passionate intensity.

Loyalty to people—to self, to friends, to family, to mankind; loyalty to ideals, convictions, causes; loyalty to institutions like the home, the school, the Church, the community, the country, the efforts to unite the world; loyalty to God—to the One in whom we live and move and have our being—life demands some kind of stand of all on such matters. When the Bible said "None of us lives to himself and none of us dies to himself," it was giving an early and profound expression to what we now call the "social nature of life." We cannot escape relationships with others and with the total world of which we are a part. That is the deepest reason why we as human beings cannot escape having loyalties of some sort or other. They may be stupid or sensible, irrational or rational, destructive or creative—but whatever they are, for better or for worse, we will have them.

Loyalty is to human life what instinct is to animal life. The life and relationships of animals are largely regulated by instincts of various kinds and, while we humans have our instincts, the really definitive thing about us is the pattern of our loyalties. It is fair to say that we do not know who we really are until we are able to say what we are loyal to, nor do we know another until we get inside of his casual tastes and interests and discover his loyalties. Then and only then can we say we know him.

All peoples have their legends and poems celebrating the glory of loyalty to friend, to country or people, and to God.

The legends of ancient Greece furnish an unforgettable story of the power of loyalty. Euripides gives it immortality in his play, *Iphigenia in Tauris*.[1] Two young men named Orestes and Pylades are shipwrecked and cast upon an unknown island. Here they are taken by the natives to the priestess in charge of the shrine. She pronounces that one of them must die and the other bear a message back to Greece for her. She decides that Pylades must die. But Orestes remonstrates; he begs her to take his life instead. He concludes his plea with these words:

> Vile is he
> Who leaves a friend in peril and goes free
> Himself. And, as it chances, this is one
> Right dear to me; his life is as my own.

Moved by his persuasion the priestess consents to let Pylades bear the message to Greece while Orestes is to die. But Pylades will have none of it. He cries out:

> I cannot live for shame if thou art dead.
> I sailed together with thee; let us die
> Together . . . Nay all ways but one
> Are shut. My last breath shall go forth with thine,
> Thy bloody sword, thy gulf of fire be mine
> Also.

In vivid contrast, superficial friendship as well as the betrayal of friendship have been the target of some of the sharpest shafts

[1] From Euripides: *Iphigenia in Tauris*, translated by Gilbert Murray. Copyright, 1910, by Oxford University Press, Inc. Used by permission.

of the poets. Shakespeare turns the spotlight on the perversion of friendship in one of his tragedies, *Timon of Athens.*

As the story opens, Timon, a wealthy man, is famous for his liberality. His friends are many. They make it a point to gather often around his table, to partake of his food, and to revel in his generosity. One day the manager of his household confronts him with the news that his money is gone, his lands are mortgaged; only his friends are left as resources. But Timon does not worry. Are not his friends both numerous and wealthy? He dispatches his servants to three of those who have been closest to him, crying, "I am wealthy in my friends."

But his servants speedily return with the news that his friends not only will not help him but, in addition, accuse him of being a wastrel. Enraged beyond words, Timon invites them all to another gala feast. They assemble gladly, chiding him for pretending that he needed to borrow from them and assuring him that they too were only pretending when they had refused to lend. But Timon is no longer deceived. He urges them to take their seats at the table and bids them eat with these cordial words: "Uncover, dogs, and lap." The astonished guests then peer into the banquet dishes and discover warm water—nothing more. Before they recover from the shock, Timon arises and shouts this ringing farewell:

> May you a better feast never behold,
> You knot of mouth-friends! Smoke and lukewarm water
> Is your perfection . . .

And as his erstwhile guests beat a hasty retreat, Timon hurls their banquet after them—dishes and all.

The lore of the Hebrew-Christian tradition is especially rich in epics dealing with loyalty and disloyalty. The friendship of Jonathan and David is one of these, dealing as it does with the loyalty of Jonathan and the disloyalty of Saul to David. Once Jonathan and David have sworn the oath of loyalty to each other, it becomes the central fact in their lives. Each is willing to pay the price for it and does so as the story unfolds. Today, when you want to describe a perfect friendship, you say, "They are like Jonathan and David."

The book of Ruth contains one of the best-known legends of loyalty. While others hang back, finally refusing to accompany Naomi to her homeland, Ruth stands firmly at her side. She both renounces her heritage and carves out a niche in immortality in that priceless affirmation of loyalty: "Entreat me not to leave thee, or to return from following after thee; for whither thou goest, I will go; and where thou lodgest, I will lodge; thy people shall be my people, and thy God my God; where thou diest, will I die, and there will I be buried: the Lord do so to me, and more also, if aught but death part thee and me."

The New Testament contains many examples of loyalty, as you know, but I want to call attention to one that may not meet the eye—the loyalty of Mark to Paul. Paul, you may recall, lost confidence in Mark early in his ministry. He refused to take him on the second missionary journey because he thought Mark had simply quit on the first one. Why Mark did quit, or whether he did, we do not know. All we know is that Paul and Barnabas split up over Mark, with Barnabas taking Mark as his companion and Paul taking Silas. Mark might have held this against Paul all his life and Paul might have refused ever to trust Mark again. But there is one eloquent line in a letter which Paul was to write many years later from one of his prisons: "Take Mark, and bring him with thee, for he is profitable to me for the ministry." There's a full comeback and complete reinstatement for you!

The 27th Psalm belongs to this rich tradition of loyalty. It deserves to be read as a hymn of loyalty to God. The writer finds the answer to the ills of life in the simple phrase: trust God and be not afraid. And he uses it steadily in his song beginning with the word, "The Lord is my light and my salvation; whom shall I fear," and ending with, "Wait for the Lord; be strong, and let your heart take courage; yea, wait for the Lord!"

III

Life demands loyalties; great religion exalts loyalty as a great virtue: that much is clear. But it does not therefore follow that creative loyalties are given to us for the asking. Every single in-

stance I have just cited to celebrate the glory of loyalty also under-
scores the costliness of it, the dangers that have to be met and
mastered if it is to remain a creative force in life. We shall not
appreciate to the full the seriousness of the demand loyalties make
on us until we face quite openly the dangers that they bring.

One of the permanent dangers of loyalty is this: little loyalties
have a way of either masquerading as great loyalties or of crowding
them out of proper place. In New Testament parlance, second
things have a way of becoming first things in this business of living.
Food and raiment become more important than the body and soul
of man. Wealth, fame and power become the chief end of man—
and when that happens his soul is required of him.

You have seen this happen; it may have happened to you; it can
happen to anyone. Here is a man who is so intent on getting ahead
in his business and professional career that he neglects his wife, his
children, his church and his larger duties in our common life. He
gives so much of his time, energy and effort to the job that he has
little of any of these for the rest of his life. Granted—and readily
enough—his wife and children and even his church may profit by
the generosity of his giving as his income increases, but there is
one thing he cannot write a check to cover: his personal influence,
his presence, his companionship, the sense of being and belonging
together that is of the essence of love, marriage, home and family.
It is an old truth: "A gift without the giver is bare."

Here is a woman—the wife of a doctor or professor, let us say—
who understandably and commendably wants to help her husband
in every way. She is so close to the home and family that she sort
of takes them for granted. She knows that they are important—if
you were to arrest her in her activities with a question about them
she would say at once that they are of greatest importance. But,
even so, she begins to spend more and more of her time and energy
joining this and belonging to that and going here in order to "meet
the right people." What happens? In the poet's words: "Things
fall apart; the center cannot hold." In Jesus' words, first things
have slipped out of perspective, giving way to second things.

Here is a young man or woman in the university seeking an education . . . Need I finish the story? Every student past or present here this morning can finish it for me. One girl left the University last fall because she was not pledged by the sorority she wanted to join. A young man was tempted to quit school because he had flunked a course and was afraid his father would think he had let him down. An athlete had a bad season on the gridiron and he planned to quit school because he thought he was a failure.

Loyalty is a great and good force in life if it is centered in first things, if it exalts in our life, thought, and dreams the ideals, ends and goals that are eternally, not just temporarily, important.

Still another danger that must be faced as we seek to answer life's demand for loyalties is this: the open conflict between and among loyalties. Ideally, loyalty to home, church, country and God should never collide with one another. But they do—and frequently. We have already seen this is the way in which they get out of order in our life. It must be faced on still another level.

I hesitate even to mention so hot an issue as the recent steel strike as an example of this conflict in loyalties. I do so because of a discerning comment on it that appears in an issue of the *Manchester Guardian* which came to this country at that time. Alistair Cooke, famed reporter of the American scene to this British paper, was summing up the claims of management and labor in the dispute. Both insist upon the full justice of their widely different positions. Both insist, further, that their position, if taken, will benefit "the country." While this is not the full case for either, it is a fair presentation of the starting point of both sides: each wants what will serve its best interests first; each is willing to have the other benefited as soon thereafter as possible; each identifies the triumph of its cause with the welfare of the country.

I cite this case because it illustrates the realistic nature of the conflict of loyalties that is found in every social, economic and political issue before us today. There is no easy answer, no pat formula, no certain road away from this kind of conflict—at least, none that I know of. The point at which I propose to leave this matter just now can be put this way: We never will solve such conflicts until we see them for what they are—conflicts between relatively limited loyalties—and try to set them in the perspective of a larger loyalty—and do it fairly.

A third danger that must be run by one who is intent on meeting life's demand for loyalties is the common notion that loyalty is blind, uncritical faith in something or someone. This is one of the most dangerous misconceptions of loyalty that could possibly invade the human mind. The writer of Proverbs would not agree with it for one moment. "Faithful are the wounds of a friend" is his way of pointing up the realistic, critical nature of personal loyalty. And I am inclined to believe that his insight applies to all forms of loyalty. If Stephen Decatur ever said "Our country! in her intercourse with foreign nations may she always be in the right; but our country, right or wrong!" and intended it to be taken as blind loyalty to country, he was dishonoring every one of the Founding Fathers of this country, as well as every great leader we have ever had. Patriotism so conceived is a one-way road to catastrophe. Loyalty to person or country does not preclude criticism; it requires and presupposes it.

I am sure every husband here joins me in the fervent hope that the criticisms of his wife are as truly expressions of her affection for him as are her praises. Love does not preclude criticism, difference of opinion, and discussions that occasionally go to the roots of the matter. Love needs that kind of understanding, that kind of assistance, if it is to make its greatest contribution to life.

So it is with our way of life, our country, our church. Loyalty to these is not blind affection; it is a complete yet critical commitment of oneself to them and willingness to work in them. "Faithful are the wounds of a friend." We need to see ourselves as others see us in order truly to see ourselves. Only one who really cares for us will take the time or be able to tell us how we are or seem to others. Criticisms born of concern and affection are among the most precious aids to loyalty we have, and we should so regard them.

IV

In the Psalmist's urging that we should set the love of God before all else; in Jesus' teaching that we should seek first the Kingdom of God we have the clue we need to advance boldly toward the loyalties we need for creative living.

Loyalty to self can yield selfishness—unless we keep firmly in mind our relationship to God the Giver of Life; the One in whose sight we hold our life in stewardship.

Loyalty to family can become a form of clannishness unless we see our family life as a medium through which God is trying to work His will for all men as well as for us.

Love of society can be a form of racism or nationalism or some economic "ism" unless we are willing to see every human institution as an imperfect instrument through which God is trying to work His perfect work in human life.

Loyalty to our Church can become a form of fanaticism unless we pray always for keen awareness of the shortcomings of the Church and for the strength to correct them. The Church may and must preach the Kingdom of God, but she never dare pretend that she is the Kingdom of God. She must always hold herself in readiness to receive such new light as may break forth from His word and His world.

Life demands loyalties and loyalties demand God. As we learn to place all lesser loyalties on the altar of supreme loyalty to God, we will discover the strong faith: Trust God and be not afraid.

VII

"With Exultation!"

SCRIPTURE LESSON: Psalm 30:1–12

I

OUR Processional Hymn, "Joyful, joyful, we adore Thee, God of Glory, Lord of Love," is both one of the best-known poems of Henry van Dyke and one of the best-loved hymns of the Christian Church. It appears in every hymnal I have seen. Glancing through the hymnal of the Evangelical and Reformed Church recently, I found the hymn, and it carries two words to indicate the tempo with which it should be sung: "With exultation!"

These words indicate more than the tempo of a great hymn; they suggest the tempo of a great religious faith. And, as such, they are our answer to the rumor, suspicion or charge that religion is essentially a gloomy business, one in which we sit around holding a glorified wake for the human race and pass the time by telling sad stories about sin, tragedy and death. As a matter of fact, the advice to live our faith "with exultation" highlights one of the oldest and strongest characteristics of great religion.

We sometimes forget that religion has produced or encouraged many if not most of the arts, particularly instrumental and vocal music and the dance. Our earliest records of Hebrew life tell of festivals—holy days—in which harp and timbrel were played as the people danced and sang their songs. The earliest services in the Temple made use of these same symbols of creative joy and confident faith. It is no accident that the Psalms, written as they were, for use in the Temple, refer constantly to music, dancing and song as tokens of religious joy.

I am sure you did not miss the strong note of great joy which resounds through the 30th Psalm which was read earlier in the service. It was written, we are told, to be sung at the dedication of the Temple itself. As the "poet laureate" of ancient Israel let his mind dwell on what he wanted to emphasize upon that historic occasion, he must have passed in review the long history of his people. He saw it

> . . . all its lights and shadows, all its wealth and all the woe.

Suffering, loss, defeat, doubts, tragedy—all these bitter facts were there, and in abundance. How much should they influence his song for the occasion? If too much, it would be a dirge, a lament, a wail, and he did not want that. He wanted a shout of joyous faith in the God who had been with them through it all, who had finally led them to this high moment! This is how he finally puts it:

> Sing unto the Lord, O ye saints of his, and give thanks at the remembrance of his holiness. For his anger endureth but a moment; in his favour is life: weeping may endure for a night, but joy cometh in the morning.

There is a realistic, joyous faith for you! Weeping, symbolizing all the woes of Israel, is a traveler sent of God, and he has been their guest overnight. But another traveler, also sent of God, and symbolizing the blessings of Israel, is on his way. He is a shout of joy; he comes at break of day, and he comes to stay!

Small wonder the swords of every great empire of antiquity blunted their edge and finally broke their blades on a faith like this. That is precisely what happened, historically. The armies of Israel were shattered, in turn, by Egypt, Assyria, Babylon, Greece and Rome, not once but repeatedly over a period of nearly a thousand years. Though they might shatter her armies, they could not shatter her faith—no matter how hard they tried. Each time defeat and adversity swept over the land, the hearts of Israel would murmur: "Weeping may endure for a night, but joy cometh in the morning."

There is a parallel to this Old Testament experience in one of the most radiant books in the New Testament—Paul's letter to the *Philippians*. Paul had been instrumental in founding the church in Philippi, and it seems to have been one of the happiest experiences he had in trying to build a church. He had gone on his way after bringing the fellowship into existence and later found himself in trouble all along the line. Some of his churches were quarreling, some of his colleagues were deserting him, he was under criticism by many, and, to top it all off, he was in prison and possibly facing execution. The church in Philippi heard of this and sent one of their number with a gift and with instructions to help him in every way possible. Paul's letter is his acknowledgment of their thoughtfulness. What a letter it is! It opens by congratulating the Philippians on their "joy in the faith." It closes with the earnest exhortation: "Rejoice in the Lord always; again I will say, Rejoice."

If Paul had wanted to moan and wail about the "slings and arrows of outrageous fortune," he could have done so and no one could have rebuked him. Instead he wrote this note that has as its keynote the single word "*Rejoice*." A Canadian scholar closes his study of the book with these words:

Written as it was under the shadow of a dark and ominous cloud, the epistle resounds with the note of joy. It is one of the priceless treasures of the Christian Church. To countless pilgrims on the way of life, it has brought comfort and strength, and it will continue so to do as long as time shall last.[1]

II

From the very beginning of our religious tradition, then, we have been singing:

Joyful, joyful we adore Thee
God of Glory, Lord of Love,

and we have been singing it "with exultation." It is a great thing to belong to a religion that keeps breaking forth in song. We ought to account it one of our greatest good fortunes that we do. Men like Palestrina, Isaac Watts, Charles Wesley, are the lineal

[1] J. Hugh Michael, in Moffatt Commentary on *Philippians*. Harper, 1927.

descendants of the Psalmist and Paul in this regard. For over two thousand years songs have been written attempting to express the religious mood of every major human situation. We have songs of sorrow, trouble, doubt, confusion, anxiety, defeat and death, as well as victory, joy and triumph. Running through them all as the thread of constant meaning is the note of strong, confident joy. Even the songs that are associated with death—songs like New-man's "Lead, Kindly Light" (which, incidentally, has suffered and survived the fate of being embalmed in a miserable tune)—even these are to be sung "with exultation."

I do not think it possible to overestimate the value of a faith that sings. For a song is a way of passing beyond the prose of reason to the poetry of emotion and feeling. A song will stir us in a way an argument never does. Even those of us who have difficulty carrying a tune in any one direction like to sing. We understand the answer a little girl gave when asked why she liked a certain song she was singing all of the time. "It makes me feel good all over," was her answer. We like to share in a service of worship where the congregation loves to sing and does so with interest and enthusiasm. While the sentiments and the tunes of some songs are much to be preferred to others, we are the poorer if we miss the note of courage, triumph and joy which runs through most of them. All are to be sung "with exultation." They should be sung that way because they celebrate a faith that ought to be lived that way.

III

I know of no way to improve on the judgment of the Catechism that "the chief end of man is to glorify God and enjoy Him forever." This points to a number of steps that we must take if we would actually grasp and live the meaning of a creative Christian life:

1. Believe in God as we see Him in Jesus Christ.
2. Have faith in the will of God.
3. Rejoice in our faith.
4. Share it with others as our most precious possession.

Though these may be stated separately they must be lived together, because together they are the contagious Christian life. Quite obviously we must believe in God and, just as obviously, we must have enough faith in Him to try to do His Will as we understand it. All, I think, would agree to this. Some would like to stop there, saying, "That is all there is to religion: believe in God and try to do His will." That is much if not most of it, I grant you, but not all. Our awareness and appreciation of what religion means to us ought to bring us alternately to our knees in prayers of gratitude and to our feet in songs of joy. It ought to create in us the desire that finds expression in a hymn still used in revival services, "Help somebody today!" What we say and do under the impulse of our religious faith ought to be done with radiance and joy.

This I know: *Joy in faith means power in life.* And it means power at points and times when we need it most.

Joy in faith means power to pursue a purpose in a day of confusion. By that standard, we need a good many more men than we seem to have these days. We are over half way on the journey toward the shameful goal of being The Century of Complete Confusion. When I speak of confusion I do not mean "change." Change is one thing—and it is both inevitable and can be good, but confusion is quite another, and it is utterly without merit. Tennyson, standing in the nineteenth century and keenly conscious of his Christian heritage, could cry out:

> Yet I doubt not thro' the ages
> One increasing purpose runs,

but that is the very thing many if not most citizens of the twentieth century do doubt. Which, as well as anything else, sums up the nature of our confusion. We are confused by cross-purposes because we are unconvinced by any one purpose; we are overwhelmed by a flood of little purposes because we are uncommitted to some one great purpose.

Look at some of the cross-purposes that paralyze us these days! And by "us" I mean each one of us personally as well as our nation and the world.

At times we believe in and know we should work for a genuine community of nations. We know that this means the surrender of certain portions of the freedom of action and sovereignty we have exercised in the past. We do not like to give up anything as important as these, but at times we are aware and almost willing to do it for the sake of avoiding war and creating some kind of world community. That we shall have to move in new directions in order to reach these goals is obvious, or should be obvious to all.

But there are other times when we want to retreat from the wisdom of that goal and the reality of sacrifices essential to its achievement. We excuse our reluctance saying, "We're not ready for it yet"; "other nations do not want it"; "other nations do not appreciate our values"—all of which have a measure of real truth in them. Buttressed by this fact, we turn tail on the original purpose and follow another until we confront the certainty of World War III—then we double-back again pleading for world community. Multiply our personal indecision by 156 million and the result is the complete confusion of the thought of this country on our role in world affairs. Multiply that result by the number of nations in the world, and you have a Century of Complete Confusion in the making.

The most alarming thing about it all is not that we are confused but that so many of us are resigned to the confusion. We have given up hoping for, believing in, and trying to find a way out of it. We simply mill around with the main drift of opinion at any given moment and hope somehow it will come out all right.

But a vital religious faith does not quit, nor does it mill around! It moves into this situation "with exultation." While it knows no easy way out, it knows that there is a way out and bids us search until we find it. It confronts cross-purposes with the fact of one purpose—God's purpose. That, at a stroke, removes the spirit of resignation and creates the consciousness of responsibility. Which is the slight difference between being an animate atom battered here and there by uncontrollable forces and being a responsible person trying to find his way in the will of God.

A number of years ago a troop of Boy Scouts went for a hike in the north woods with an old woodsman. He purposely let them get themselves gloriously lost. It was some time before they realized that they were lost, and when they did, they held high and fearful debate as to the right direction. Finally they turned to the old guide who had been listening quietly to the discussion. He said, "We got in and we can get out. All we've got to do is to get our sense of direction and then find a trail that leads the way we want to go." The advice was good even though carrying it out involved hours of hard work.

We too need a sense of direction and the confidence we can find a trail that leads the way we want to go. This is the contribution of great faith, and we can get it from no other source. It converts a baffled person into a human being with purpose. It converts a milling mob into a community of colleagues in a great undertaking. It converts a congregation of hundreds or even thousands of individuals into a church dedicated to the glorification and the achievement of the great purpose—the Kingdom of God. While it does not present us with a detailed road map into the future such as the A. A. A. furnishes travelers, it does give us a sense of direction and confidence enough to take it in company with others. It gives us a faith in God, in His will, in others and in ourselves, and bids us find our way therein "with exultation." It asks us to empower our purpose with confidence and joy. It asks us to share our faith with others as our most priceless possession.

IV

Joy in faith means power in life! Few things can cut us down quicker than despair and the feeling of futility in our life or in our work. Not many of us live long without having to do battle with these enemies of the creative spirit, and we would do well to realize that a joyous faith is our most reliable weapon in the battle.

The way some of us live makes you ashamed to belong to the human race. I am referring not alone to those who break the laws of God and man and distort, pervert and destroy every human value and relationship they touch. I am referring, too, to people who live on the downbeat all of the time, who moan and wail their way wearily from one day to the next, who can hear the laughter of little children and not feel their pulse quicken, who can pass through all of the beauty that God has lavished on this earth without ever seeing it, much less being strengthened by it, who can see men in great trouble and can only think to say, "Just let me tell you about my operation." People like that give the lie all unthinkingly to the faith that "This is my Father's world—I rest me in the thought."

Then there are others who make you proud yet humble to belong to the human family. They are the ones who have known difficulty, doubt, defeat, sorrow, but who have overcome them. They have faced these difficulties with the faith that under God and with His help they could be managed and mastered. People like this roll back the horizons of our narrow selfish lives. We see ourselves as God intends us to be—sensitive, creative members of His family sharing our lives with one another. Lives of people like this are blessed by a contagious faith and they live it with exultation.

I have seen this enormous difference between qualities of lives translated many times but never more vividly than in these few situations.

The first contrast occurred in a Negro church on the South Side during my student days at the University of Chicago. A panel of speakers consisting of Charles Gilkey of the University Chapel, Clarence Darrow, and two other speakers were addressing a church packed with people—mostly colored. The depression was at its worst at that time; money and jobs were scarce, and the morale of everyone was on the floor. Clarence Darrow took advantage of that fact to point out the plight of the Negroes. He summed up their woes, concluding, "And yet you sing! No one can sing like you do! What do you have to sing about?" Quick as a flash a Negro lady in the congregation shouted, "We've got Jesus to sing about!" For once Darrow was stopped dead in his tracks. He was face to face with one who had faith in the fact that "weeping may endure for a night, but joy cometh in the morning."

The other contrast is between two men, one relatively modern, the other an ancient. Sir Edmund Gosse, a famous British critic and writer of the nineteenth century, had lost his ancestral faith and had not thought it important to seek another. The longer he lived the less confidence he actually had in the value and meaning of life. Finally he wrote these mournful lines:

> The Past is like a funeral gone by,
> The Future comes like an unwelcome guest.

Now look at the other man—Paul. He, too, had lost his ancestral faith, but he had taken the trouble to find another, and it swells up with exultation as he faces the future, "For I am sure that neither death, nor life, nor angels, nor principalities, nor things present, nor things to come, nor powers, nor heights, nor depths, nor anything else in all creation, will be able to separate us from the love of God in Christ Jesus our Lord." Don't believe for a moment that a vibrant, creative, religious faith doesn't make all the difference in the world!

We cannot inherit the faith we need for a life like that. It does not come to us through the germ plasm. No one can hand it to us for the asking. We must fight for it with all our mind, heart, soul and strength, and once we get it, in order to be true to it, even to keep it, we must share it with others as our most precious possession. Try to husband it in a selfish way and we will lose it every time. It must be shared to be enjoyed, and it must be enjoyed to be shared! It will be our one purpose in a world of cross-purposes, our great purpose in a world of little purposes, but it is worth every moment of time, every ounce of energy we put into it—and much more—because with and through it the lights come up, and a shout of joy echoes all through life. Then each of us in his own way is able to say: "Weeping may endure for a night, but joy cometh in the morning." "Rejoice in the Lord always; again I will say, Rejoice." As Christians, we have something to rejoice in, something to sing about, something to share. Let us then, under God, be about it daily as the most important thing we can do. And let us do it with exultation!

VIII

Truth is the Banner

SCRIPTURE LESSON: Psalm 60:1–4; 61:1–8

I

AS A MAN approaches the witness stand in our courts he is greeted with the question, "Do you solemnly swear to tell the truth, the whole truth, and nothing but the truth, so help you God?" When he says "Yes," he moves into a totally different life situation. Gone is the pleasant freedom of ordinary behavior, gone are the random words and little asides that form so large a part of his ordinary speech. Every word must now be weighed with great care. He is under oath, under law in a special way and with a specially assumed obligation before God and man to tell the truth as he sees it. While in the chair he must expect to have his testimony examined and cross-examined as it is made and becomes a factor in reaching a decision.

Generations, even ages, are forced to take the witness stand and hear the Lord of Life and History put the question, "Do you solemnly swear to tell the truth, the whole truth, and nothing but the truth?" This is what happened not alone to the Hebrews in the Old Testament and the Christians in the New Testament, but also in all great moments of Christian history. It is one of the deepest meanings of what we so glibly call "a religious experience." Look for a moment at the experience of the Hebrews and Christians on the witness stand before we take it ourselves. Their experience may help us through the inevitable ordeal of our generation.

The Hebrews would be the first to assure us that it is a difficult assignment to take the witness stand of history. Yet that is precisely what they did to their eternal glory and to the permanent enrichment of mankind. They felt called of God to take the witness stand, there to tell the truth, the whole truth, and nothing but the truth about the will of God for the life of man as they understood it. The Old Testament is a brilliant but far from complete record of some fifteen hundred years on the witness stand, during which the Hebrews gave testimony and were subjected to the cross-examination of their own experience as well as that of their neighbors.

Dip into this record anywhere, and we will discover a people under oath, with a sense of peculiar obligation before God and man. In their own words, they were under covenant with God. Usually known as "the chosen people" they might as well be called "the sworn people," "the committed people"—sworn and committed to tell the whole truth about the meaning of God for man. The Psalms that were read earlier in this service ring with a sense of obligation. They furnish a lucid insight into the vigorous notion of truth and truth-telling that runs through our Bible from one end to the other. For the Psalmist feels that God has done more than put words in their mouth; He has thrust a banner in their hands—a banner that they are to display and under which they are to march. *"Thou hast given a banner to them that fear thee, that it may be displayed because of the truth."*

The Hebrews accepted this banner and it became the distinctive thing about them. They centered their thoughts, their hopes and their dreams in it; they organized their entire life around it; they displayed it with courage and pride to everyone—Egyptian, Assyrian, Babylonian, Greek and Roman.

And well they might display it! It was their soul, their purpose, their witness to the world, and they believed that their testimony pointed the way of life to all mankind. Prophet and priest alike were trying to get men to face a few simple facts that told the truth about life: (1) God exists. (2) His will for the world is the truth of the world. (3) Man must find his way in that will if he would live. God and truth were inseparable ideas for the Hebrews. Loyalty to God was loyalty to the truth, and loyalty to truth was loyalty to God. He who discovers something new about truth has discovered something new about God.

Amos, for example, studying the ebb and flow of historical events, discovered this new truth about history: All life is governed by moral law. He saw at once that it added something new to the existing idea of God. Instead of being the God of the Hebrews, he was the God of all mankind; he was the moral law which bound all men together in history. The brightest pages of the Old Testament were written by men like Amos who not only made such discoveries but who felt obligated by God to share them with their fellows. Over and over again in every age and with all varieties of emphasis this banner of the truth of God was lifted by the Hebrews; it was their testimony to the whole truth of the meaning of God for man as they understood it.

II

The New Testament, like the Old, was written by and about men who felt that they were sworn of God to tell the whole truth about the meaning of God for man. Agreeing with everything their Hebrew ancestors had said, they made one all-important addition. They agreed that God exists, that His will for the world is the truth of the world, that man can find life only by finding his way in that will. Then they added this: we have our perfect revelation of the will of God for the life of man in the life and teachings of Jesus Christ. He fulfills the Law and the Prophets of our fathers, and by fulfilling them he transcends them. Therefore we must follow him.

The Gospel of John might well be called the Gospel of Truth. For it is especially emphatic in its presentation of Jesus as the Truth of God. And it is equally emphatic in its presentation of Christian discipleship as an adventure in truth. Not only does Jesus say, "I am the truth," he calls upon men to worship God in spirit and in truth. He challenges his disciples with what William Lyon Phelps once called the greatest verse in the Bible: "Ye shall know the truth, and the truth will make you free." His final prayer for his disciples contains this revealing petition: "Consecrate them in the truth."

This then is the banner of truth which the Christian faith has displayed from the very beginning. Truth, so conceived, is much deeper than mere obedience to law, than mastering a catechism and being able to rattle it off at will. Truth, for the historic Christian faith, is a total personal relationship with God, involving every faculty we have—mind, body, spirit; involving every relationship with others we have or hope to have.

The Christian faith has always invited men to seek and find God. It has never asked them to move under the impulse of blind faith. For God, the God of the universe, can be known. When thunderstruck Jew and Greek listeners demanded to know how God can be known, the answer came at once. The truth of God can be seen and known not alone in the handiwork of the Creator in the universe round about us, but pre-eminently in Jesus Christ. If you really want to know the full meaning of the truth of God you must know Jesus Christ. "He that hath seen me hath seen the Father." Approach Jesus Christ with singleness of mind, purity of conscience, and openness of heart, and you will discover the truth of God—this was the faith of the early Church.

Knowing the truth, in this sense, is far more than a mastery of abstract principles or ideas; it is an actual participation with our whole life in the life of God. The fruit of this kind of participation can be summed up in three words: freedom, purpose and power. The early Church shows what happens when these words come alive in the lives of men.

Those early Christians looked at the world with new eyes. They felt free to examine their entire life in the light of the truth of God which they found in Jesus Christ. They felt free to reject the parts of hallowed tradition that seemed to distort or deny this truth. They felt free to challenge the pagan gods and philosophies of Greece and Rome with this truth. They felt free to defy the Roman Emperor as well as local authorities who tried to make them play down or renounce this truth. They felt free to turn their backs on their homelands and set their eyes on the far horizons of the world, that men everywhere might learn of the truth of God in Christ. And, in each of these terribly difficult situations and decisions, they found the power to see it through. For the truth of God is the power of God as well—this is the living witness of their life.

III

This, in all too brief form, is the banner which we receive in our religious heritage. Like the great seal of Harvard University, it has the single word *Veritas* inscribed on it. We are invited to take it in the spirit of the Psalmist; that is, as from God Himself: "Thou hast given a banner to them that fear thee, that it may be displayed because of the truth."

How I wish I could report that modern man is eager to receive and display this banner! But such is not the case. In fact, three powerful tendencies in our life today threaten religion's historic allegiance to this banner. Look at them for a moment. I do hope you do not discover yourself among them!

First, there are the relativists who disbelieve in truth. Like Pilate, they want to know "What is truth?" and you can tell by the way they ask the question they think there is no answer to it. For half a century now a new movement in contemporary philosophy has been arguing that truth is a convenience, a fiction, that all it can mean is this: I want something badly. When I say I seek the truth what I really mean is that I set up as a goal for life something I want, and then I call it by the hallowed name of truth.

No one can say how influential this relativism is going to be, but it has much to answer for already. It is coming home to roost in the various forms of moral bankruptcy that are plaguing us today. We are experiencing a moral bankruptcy so complete that many people are inclined to treat honor, truth and virtue as mid-Victorian jokes. I once heard the dean of a college of liberal arts in a great university openly complain of the trouble modern education is having with the moral absolutes of historic religion. "They don't make sense any more," he said, "yet many students cling to them." I answered, in effect, "I've got news for you: Your troubles have just begun. We're trying to raise up a generation of men and women who will seek, honor and love the absolute truth of Almighty God and find the moral commitments of their lives therein!"

A second group among us who are reluctant to grasp the banner of truth that we have received from our fathers are those who believe in the supremacy of something else—church, state, race or social order. They hold these little coins so close to their eyes that they shut out the sun of God's truth. They not only believe that their church is *the* church, their race *the* race, their form of society *the* society, they are prepared to defend their convictions against all comers. Understandably they are on their guard against those who are out simply to make trouble. But, quite dangerously, they lump all critics together and put them in the category of heretics, traitors or subversives. They stone prophets and traitors alike; they crucify Christ and criminals at one and the same time and in the same manner—and call it a good day's work.

These people are the supporters of the Senator McCarthys of this and every other age. They are not scheming, malicious men out to destroy truth; they are frightened, angry men trying to protect the truth in our way of life. But their fears and hates have blinded them to the meaning of the truth they seek to serve. They are a little like the trained bear who loved his master so much he could not see anything hurt him. Seeing a fly on his beloved trainer's brow, and hating the fly for being there, he grabbed a stone and threw it at the fly with all his might. It is recorded that he hit the fly.

This spirit loves the truth, but it neither understands nor serves it well. Truth has its own nature—and he who would serve truth must be willing to follow it. Truth opens out on an unlimited horizon. It points down a road that runs over the hills of eternity. Those we have been describing want none of it. But even as they reject it they should confront certain facts. Try insulating life from growth, and death sets in. Try insulating social forms from the criticisms necessary to growth, and death sets in. Write it down as an axiom of human experience: He who subordinates loyalty to truth to loyalty to anything else will not only deny and disown truth eventually but will finally lose the things he puts ahead of truth.

A third group among us who are worried about this banner of truth are guided by counsels of prudence. They believe in truth, right enough, but they think that we are living in such dangerous days that we need to settle for what we can safely get. They cast a worried glance at the New Testament pronouncement, "Ye shall know the truth, and the truth will make you free," thinking it a dangerous utterance. Then, looking at academic freedom, they say, "Fine in principle, but in actual practice it must be closely guarded by loyalty oaths, etc." The oath of loyalty for citizenship is not enough for these frightened people. We must have something more, they say. So in the name of preserving freedom they curtail it in practice; and by putting fear at the hearts of the men who need freedom, in order to let it be creative and growing, they tend to kill the love of it. And, lest we forget, the successful curtailment of freedom in one area will lead to similar efforts in all other areas. The great freedoms of life stand or fall together.

IV

A number of years ago an Old Testament scholar was publishing a radical theory of the authorship of the book of Isaiah, and he admitted that he shrank from the hail of criticism that was sure to follow. But, he said, "there is a worse fate than being misunderstood; it is to be to truth a timid friend." That word I would lift in warning to all who for whatever reason are tempted to lower the banner of truth in these difficult days. We in churches have never lowered it without regretting our action. Look at the sorry record of our efforts as a church to limit the growth of the sciences. Look at the record of intolerance and persecution which blackens the history of every major religious body when we are tempted to lose faith in the search for truth and to limit freedom.

As I study these tendencies to lower the banner of truth today, I am reminded of what the French critic, Vinet, once wrote: "Most friends of truth love it as Frederick the Great loved music.

It used to be said of him that, strictly speaking, he was not fond of music but of the flute, and not indeed fond of the flute but of his flute." It is a sad and tragic thing when our love of truth is confined to our own flute.

We have too great a heritage in the banner of, and witness for, truth to display it with shaking hands and faltering faith. We have no reason to be ashamed of it; we have every reason to be proud of it. It is our soul, our witness, our purpose as Christians and as a Church.

Loyalty to the truth of God is the great loyalty of life. It is deeply personal in the exact sense that no one can force us into it, nor can they take it from us. We embrace it from choice and conviction or not at all. But when we do, it becomes one of the most important public facts about us. It tells people where we stand and what we stand for in life. Because of it, more than anything else, men will treat us as friend or foe. What better differential could we ask?

I do not think there was ever a more opportune time than now for the Christian Church to reaffirm her ancient allegiance to the truth of God, to lift the historic banner of truth in her thought and life, to encourage her members and institutions everywhere to do likewise. This is no time for Christians to "be to truth a timid friend"; it is the time for vigorous, tough-minded loyalty to the truth of God which is the unfolding purpose of the universe in which we are trying to find our way. And the Church should make known her loyalty in such unmistakable terms that the embattled forces of freedom the world over will know that a powerful champion has taken the field. Nor will we be cowed by the atomic blasts now shattering the structures of yesterday's world beyond repair because of our faith in, and commitment to, the God of Truth.

The Church is the symbol of loyalty to the truth of God in the life of man. The Church is on the witness stand of history sworn to tell the whole truth about the meaning of life as she sees it in Jesus Christ. Make no mistake about it: our witness will be listened to if given with sincerity and conviction. It can easily tip the balances in favor of greater faith in freedom as we face the future. Once we accept this as our duty as Christians today, we, like the early Christians, will look at our world with new eyes. We will feel free to examine our entire life in the light of the truth of God which we find in Jesus Christ. We will feel free to reject the parts of hallowed tradition that seem to distort or deny this truth. We will feel free to challenge the pagan gods and philosophies of the twentieth century with this truth. We will feel free to defy dictators and majorities alike who try to make us play down or renounce this truth. We will feel free to lift our eyes to the far horizons of the world and go there, that all men may know of this truth.

Lifting the banner of truth, we remind ourselves and say to all others: Man is the child of God—and must be regarded and treated accordingly; we are brothers one of another—and must learn to conduct ourselves accordingly, living without pride, hatred, deceit and mistrust; together we can build a new world—a world wherein men will dwell in brotherhood and peace. Every problem that stands in the way of the building of this new world is our problem; we accept it as a Christian responsibility, and we do so echoing the conviction of Arthur Hugh Clough:

> It fortifies my soul to know
> That, though I perish, Truth is so;
> That, howsoe'er I stray and range,
> Whate'er I do, Thou dost not change.
> I've steadier step when I recall
> That, if I slip, Thou dost not fall.

IX

His Hand is Firm

‣‣

SCRIPTURE LESSON: Psalm 62

I

ONE of the most influential discoveries man ever made about God was of His firmness, His dependability. It is now so much a part of our thinking about God that we take it for granted. But it was not always so—as any student of religions or even of the Old Testament knows. There was a time when the gods in whom men believed were thought to be capricious, willful, vindictive; as unstable as the sea in storm, as undependable as the four winds.

There is more than a trace of this early attitude in the story of Moses' call to return to Egypt to lead his people to freedom. The divine directive was plain enough: "The Lord said . . . 'Go back to Egypt. . . .' So Moses took his wife and his sons . . . and went back. . . ." Then there occurred this disturbing incident, "At a lodging place on the way the Lord met him and sought to kill him." And he would have done so had he not been foiled by some quick thinking and vigorous action by Moses' wife.

That incident, rough with all the tokens of primitive life and faith, stands in vivid contrast to the faith in the firmness, the dependability of God which shines through the 62nd Psalm. The writer of this Psalm deserves to be described as one who "was despised and rejected by men; a man of sorrows and acquainted with grief," yet, withal, a man of steady faith in God.

The more we study this little biographical gem the more highly we are likely to esteem its author. Life had been rich, full, but hard on him. So far as we can see, he had no illusions about life. Riches,

87

fame, power—these he saw, and saw through for the rank impostors they are. Whatever meaning life has must come from other sources. He was sick as well as surrounded by hostile people bent on his destruction. In short, he was caught up in a combination of circumstances that usually finishes off faith for all too many of us. But not for the Psalmist—his faith was made of sterner stuff.

Over against the bitter experiences of illness and enmity, he put his personal experiences of God's presence, power and love. When he did this he found his answer to illness and enmity. Not as to why they had happened to him, but as to how to face and manage them, how to live with them without being broken by them. His testament of faith is as stirring a document as we find in the Bible:

> For God alone my soul awaits . . .
> He only is my rock, . . . my fortress . . .
> I shall not be greatly moved.
> I shall not be shaken . . .
> My refuge is in God.

What wouldn't we give to have a faith like that? To be able to face the unknown future with quiet confidence instead of dark foreboding? To be able to meet misunderstanding, adversity and tragedy with poise, peace and purpose? To be able to face the certainty of suffering, loss and death with calmness of mind and spirit? To be able to cry with Edwin Markham:

> I lift my hands to the years ahead
> And cry, "Come on! I'm ready for you!" [1]

Of course it would be a wonderful thing to have a faith like that, and any sensible person knows it. But how do we get it—that bouyant faith in the firmness of God?

If there were a quick answer and an easy way, all would have it by nightfall—that we know. But the only answer we can honestly make is a careful one, and the only way we know is a most difficult one. That should not surprise us. We do not stumble on a faith like that of the Psalmist. If ever we get it or anything approaching

[1] From Edwin Markham, *New Poems: Eighty Songs at Eighty*. Copyright, 1932, by Edwin Markham. Used by permission of Virgil Markham.

it, we earn it. We pay for it in the coin of our keenest thinking, our most sensitive insights, and our most courageous ethical efforts.

Look for a moment at the three chief sources of the Psalmist's notion of the firmness of God.

II

To begin with, he saw the firmness of God in the fact of Creation. He saw God, the handiwork of God, all around him in the created universe. It never occurred to him that any serious element of chance might have entered into the world—it was God's world: made according to His holy will and purpose; done in His own way.

The Psalmist drank all this in with his mother's milk; he could never remember a time when the awesome account of creation was not a part of the thought and life of his home. The 62nd Psalm began to take form when a little Jewish lad heard his parents and elders repeat:

"And God said, 'Let there be light,' and there was light. . . .

"And God said, 'Let the waters . . . be gathered together in one place and let the dry land appear.' And it was so.

"And God said, 'Let there be light . . . to separate the day from the night. . . .' And it was so.

"And God said, 'Let us make man in our image, after our likeness . . .' So God created man in his own image, in the image of God he created him.

"And God saw everything that he had made, and, behold, it was very good."

Omar Khayyám, confronted by puzzles, problems and suffering, might sing:

> Into this Universe, and *Why* not knowing
> Nor *Whence*, like water, willy-nilly flowing;
> And out of it, as Wind along the Waste,
> I know not *Whither*, willy-nilly blowing.

I say Omar might react this way, but not one reared on the sweeping insights of Genesis—such a one would not and he did not permit his personal difficulties to blot out the tremendous fact that he was a child of God.

Leo Baeck, one of Judaism's greatest scholars, once wrote that "the consciousness of being created" by God is one of the characteristics of Judaism both ancient and modern. The Psalmist, despite the illness and enmity that surrounded him, "knew himself to have been created by God, created just as everything else had been created. His life, and all life round him, thus became for him the revelation of the One God. . . ." This was the massive fact that enabled him to lift his eyes beyond his personal troubles and proclaim:

> For God alone my soul waits . . .
> He only is my rock, . . . my fortress . . .
> I shall not be shaken.

And in the saying of it, something of the firmness of the Creator of all came into his life as a steadying, strengthening influence.

The Psalmist had still another source of confidence in the firmness of God: the traditions of his people. The Jews deserve to be called "the God-intoxicated people." God had been to them a pillar of cloud by day and a pillar of fire by night on their long and trying pilgrimage in history. More than a thousand years of that history stretched back of the Psalmist as he wrote. God had guided his fathers over that long period by and through law. He did not coddle them; He made them toe the mark of their agreement; He made them live up to their covenant. And when they failed to do so, they felt the power of His judgment.

Students of Hebrew life and law tell us that the Biblical records contain several codes of law which were drawn up at widely different times in their history—some early, some very late. Understandably, these codes differ in many ways. But not in one—for all of them, His hand is firm! The God who spoke to the needs of nomadic life as well as the One who made His will known to a settled people confronted both with a claim, an expectation, a commandment. If much were to be given to them, then much was to be required of them. This fact was clearly understood by

the great leaders of the Hebrews from the very beginning of their
life.

The great prophets of ancient Israel—all of whom had lived and
made their mark long before the age of the Psalmist—had etched
the reality of the moral law on the consciousness of Israel in im-
perishable terms. The God in whom they believed was One whose
moral law was as steady and as dependable as the fact of creation
itself. Job's wife might suggest this drastic remedy for illness,
"Curse God and die," but not one nurtured on the long tradition
of the steady goodness of God.

Hence the Psalmist's confidence in the justice of God. Whether
he regarded his illness and enmity as punishment we do not know,
and it does not much matter; he was certain that in God he could
find the strength needed to manage them. Just as the justice of
God had punished a sinful nation until it was purified, then had
restored it to its homeland; just so He could be expected to deal
with individual men. The Psalmist was neither asking nor expect-
ing personal favors as he faced his problems; he was content with
the even-handed justice of God in the affairs of men. What was
happening to him had happened and would continue to happen
to nations, to kings, to priests, as well as to ordinary people.

Most of us will admit that the Psalmist was a long sea mile
ahead of us in this matter of the firmness of His moral law. We
want God to be firm with others, but on the lenient side with us.
We want Him to show His even-handed justice to other evildoers,
but we want His mercy, His forgiveness. We are like the now-
famous man who sought out a young attorney and asked if he
would handle his case. The attorney said he would, then added,
"I'll see that you get justice." In high alarm his client cried, "I
don't want justice—I want to win."

When we feel the firmness, the steadiness, the even-handedness
of God on us bringing us under judgment, we are like the frightened American in Hermann Hagedorn's poem, *The Bomb That
Fell on America.*[2] Cringing under God's indictment, he cried,

[2] Copyright, 1946, 1950, by Hermann Hagedorn. Reprinted by permission
of the author.

"Me, Lord? . . . How odd! I'm sure you must be mistaken. There's nothing the matter with *me*. It's the other fellow that's the trouble, a hundred and thirty-five million of him.

· · · · · · · · · ·

The Lord said not a word . . .
I felt a Hand on my collar, a hand that made me remember
The woodshed and the shingle, and the glint in a father's eye.

· · · · · · · · · ·

The Lord bent over me as a mother bends over a baby.
"You are a child," said the Lord, "and
My heart is sick with your childness.
But you have a soul, and I've found you just never can tell.
If I could get by your ego and somehow crack open your nucleus—
Something might happen . . . And there is a world at stake.

God had gotten by the ego of the Psalmist; He had cracked open his nucleus! To believe in God, is to believe that He is in charge of the over-all direction of life. To revere God is to have faith that His will for the world has in it a very special place for each person. And the Psalmist revered Him! There is not the least trace of a whine in his assertion:

> For God alone my soul waits . . .
> He only is my rock, . . . my fortress . . .
> I shall not be shaken.

Those moving words ring with still another kind of confidence in the firmness of God: the Love of God. The Psalmist tells us that he has experienced not alone the power of God but even more the love of God.

"But he is sick; he is surrounded by enemies—what then can he mean by the love of God? If God loved him, why all these things?" That is what we want to know, isn't it?

There probably is no final answer to questions like these, but several things ought to be said about them. The love of God must mean something vastly greater than what we usually mean by it. I'm afraid we use it in an almost trivial way, thinking it means that God is running around like a celestial valet with no other desire than to anticipate and meet our every need. Even if we did not put it in just those terms that is about what we mean.

We need to take to heart the lesson taught by an eleven-year-old boy in a Sunday School class. The teacher was asking "Think questions" of the children upon this particular occasion. She asked, "Is there anything that God can't do?" All but this boy gave the expected answer, "No." He puzzled over it for a moment and finally said, "Yes." The teacher thinking he had misunderstood the question, asked it again, "I asked if there was anything that God could not do." "Yes ma'am, there is," he answered most emphatically. "Well, what is it?" she wanted to know. "He can't please everybody," was the reply.

Whatever else the love of God may mean, it does not mean that He is committed to the impossible task of trying to please everybody. It does mean—and this is a quite different thing—that He is actively seeking the welfare of all men; that His concern and compassion are for all men in every walk and circumstance of life.

The Psalmist had such faith in the love of God that he knew it was the source of his ability to face illness and enmity with courage and peace. His problems did not separate him from the love of God; they made him all the more dependent upon it. His devotion to God was not conditional upon his getting his way in all things; it grew out of his faith that God was trying to help him find his way. That is why he could affirm, "God is my refuge. I shall not be shaken."

III

The cynic among us will certainly jump on that word "refuge," saying that it admits that religion is an escape from the realities of life, an opiate which dulls our awareness of the real problems we face; that it is, in short, an ostrichlike process of burying our heads in the sand.

Not so fast there! Let us look at these two meanings of "refuge" before we complete that condemnation!

For one thing, refuge does mean a place to hide, to find shelter. For the other, it means a place to make a final stand; it is a strong

point, the strongest of all strong points where we try to regroup
our scattered forces for another battle. It is the contention of historic religion that faith in God is a refuge in both these senses and
that we need them—one as badly as the other.

All of us have known people who need a sanctuary, a shelter, a
place to hide and to find rest from the storms for awhile. I've
known them, and so have you—people who are literally defeated,
disorganized, unable to plan, unable to work.

Here is a middle-aged businessman who has lost his job as a
result of gross injustice. He is a pool of bitterness and every creative effort and relationship is being dragged into that pool and
drowned. He needs what? A crusade? Not at all—at least not now.
What he needs is a kind of spiritual hospitalization that will enable
him to get his life in its proper perspective once more. Then, perhaps, the crusade!

Here is a young man—a victim of acute alcoholism. Family,
friends, job—all drifting away in the drunken fogs that keep envel-
oping him. When he is sober, he is one mass of remorse, willing to
do anything to make retribution, but unable to carry through.
Does he need a crusade? Not now. But he does need a sanctuary,
a sense of deepening kinship with God which will give him the
spiritual strength he needs to bring order into his disordered life.

Here is a family who have been on the anvil of suffering for
years. First, they lost their only girl. Then they lost their business
and moved to another part of the country to start over again. By
dint of the hardest kind of hard work, they got a foothold of
security and life had begun to look up. Then—they learned that
the husband was stricken with throat cancer. Three weeks after
learning of this, they were notified that one of their boys had been
killed in training in Korea.

I ask you, what does this little family need? A crusade for a new
world order? Not now. They need a sense of the enfolding, sus-
taining, strengthening love of God—an awareness of the power, the
firmness, the steadiness of His love for them. What they need
most is what they have in God—a sanctuary, a sacred place, a place
where they may find shelter, healing and simple spiritual rest. How

long will it take before they have regrouped their scattered spiritual strength and are ready to move out again into the wider responsibilities of our life and times? Only God knows—and it must be left strictly to Him.

It is, then, without any apology or flinching that we affirm that God is our refuge, the One to whom we turn when overwhelmed by the storms of life, the One whose constant, steadfast, strengthening love is ready and sufficient for all who seek His shelter.

We affirm, too, that He is the One through whom we regroup our forces for another battle, the One in whom we take our places for a final stand against the onslaughts of life. He is the One in the bosom of whose love we find the strength we need for the tasks ahead.

Do you recall the great moment in William Saroyan's book and motion picture, *The Human Comedy?* The boys were on the troup train speeding to the port of embarkation for war and as they rolled along, one boy suggested that they sing some old hymns—hymns they all knew. "Which one?" the song leader wanted to know. "Well—that one about leaning." "Leaning?" "Yes, leaning on the Everlasting Arms!" And how they sang it—this group of men reaching back into their heritage in search of the strength they needed to dispel fear and loneliness and be ready for what lay ahead.

Whitehead's summary of the three certainties of life men need for effective living comes to mind in connection with this notion of the firmness of God. We need to believe that

1. There is a power behind the world.
2. There is a difference between right and wrong.
3. Right deserves our unquestioning allegiance.

Not only do we need these certainties, but religion has found them through faith in God. When we speak of the firmness of God, then, we are not escaping from life, we are getting squared away for the most effective, creative living open to us. What will it mean, spelled out, you ask. These things for sure:

1. A general attitude of confidence in life and in the Creator of life.

2. An attitude of trust in moments of uncertainty.
3. An attitude of love in moments of loss and disaster.

IV

Men personally have always needed and so far as we can see will always need this kind of confidence in life and in the Giver of life. And in addition we will confess, will we not, that if ever a generation needed the spiritual steadiness that comes from faith in the firmness of God, we are that generation?

With one marriage in three failing to make the grade, to whom and to what do we turn for remedy? To the psychiatrist? In some cases, yes. To the marriage counsellors? In many cases, yes. But in every case, we need to recapture our awareness of the spiritual foundations of life and marriage. Do this, and marriage is no longer at the mercy of whims and impulse; it becomes a rich shared adventure in living which proceeds steadily toward its fulfillment in home and family. Any successful remedy for the shameful ratio between marriage and divorce will begin somewhere in this area of new spiritual steadiness in our homes.

We are belatedly aroused about the dangers of juvenile delinquency in our time. And well we might be. Where laws are defective, they should be remedied. Where courts are inadequate they should be strengthened. All this and much more can undoubtedly be done—but the most important remedial measure of all is far from novel: To sense, to believe in, to build squarely on the sacredness of our homes. They are sanctuaries—places where the love of God speaks to us and through us—as truly as this room where we are now assembled. Let children grow to maturity in this steady atmosphere of love, honor, respect and devotion to God—and they will face temptation and trial feeling—perhaps saying—"For God alone my soul waits. . . . I shall not be shaken."

The firmness of God comes home to the peoples of the earth with special force and poignancy today. Despite our loud patriotic talk about being a favored nation, a favored people, we know that God plays no favorites among us. Try as we may to keep our world split up into actually or potentially warring segments, we know we shall fail. God has laid it down as an unalterable moral law that we stand or fall together. He has laid it down in His merciful love, extended evenly and steadily to all men, that we can live as brothers, that together and under Him we can live, not die, and in living share with Him in the building of a new world.

It is fitting that we should on this day recall those who are dead and give thanks for the sacrifices they made. But I am persuaded that they, if they could speak, would want us rather to anticipate the generations to come and by our sacrifices fall to the task of building the kind of world where men will beat their swords into ploughshares, their spears into pruning hooks, and would not make war any longer. To do this—we shall need to have faith in the One who is our Refuge, the One through whom we shall not be shaken —the God and father of all.

X

Where Evil is Evil!

▗▄▄▄▄▄▄▄▄▄▄▄▄▄▄▄▄▄▄▄▄▄▄▄▄▄▄

SCRIPTURE LESSON: Psalm 73:1–28 (A.V.)

TEXT: When I thought to know this, it was too painful for me; until
I went into the sanctuary of God; then I understood their
end.

I

WHENEVER I read the 73rd Psalm I find myself wanting to
make it required reading for at least two kinds of people: those
who reject religion as futile; and those whose religion does not
mean much to them or to anyone else. The first have missed the
meaning of religion altogether; the second are losing their grip on
it. It is safe to assume that not many of you here this morning
belong to the first class—those who honestly believe that religion is
of little or no value in life. People who think this are not in church,
as a rule—at least they are not here often enough to know what it
is all about. They are playing golf or picnicking and possibly telling
themselves that they are just as religious—and usually they say that
they are more so—than those of us who are simple-minded enough
to go to church.

Whatever their rationalization, there is no point talking to
people who are not here. It would be unwise to spend time with
their problem when so many of us here are in or are periodically
tempted to slide into the second group—those whose religious faith
does not mean very much to us. We have not lost it altogether, but
it no longer grips us as once it did or as we know it should. We
continue to come to church but more from habit than from eager

98

expectancy that here in fellowship with one another we shall find God. We recite the creed, share in the songs and prayers, listen to the sermon, yet feel that somehow our religious faith has lost both its radiance and its power to help us with the many moral problems both large and small that we must face each day.

What is even more to the point—and to put it bluntly—we find ourselves wondering whether religion pays, whether it actually lives up to its fine promises and tremendous assurances. Irreligious or at best casually religious people seem to be getting along beautifully —and without the inner torment of tension between high ideals and practical problems. Who can help appreciating the state of mind of Alfred E. Smith upon a certain occasion when he was a member of a fishing party somewhere in New England? His devotion to his faith led him and several fellow Catholics to roll out of bed at an early hour to go to Mass and as they tiptoed by their slumbering non-Catholic companions, Smith was heard to mutter, "Wouldn't it be awful if it turned out they were right!" Actually the experience recorded in the 73rd Psalm begins—but does not end—with some such feeling.

I wish I could have known the writer of the 73rd Psalm. He sounds like a good neighbor and friend. He was human, honest and devout. And he was having the same kind of trouble with his religion that we have with ours: It had run out of power. He had not forsaken the faith of his fathers; but he no longer got guidance, strength and comfort from it. He had reached the point where, so far as he could see, many of its counsels were in error, many of its promises untrue. Having made this appalling discovery, he felt honor-bound to proclaim rather than to hide it.

For example, he had been taught that the righteous prosper while the wicked suffer. That, he says, is not the way I see the facts. The wicked prosper; they sleep well; they have power, wealth and respect; they do as they please; and they die in peace. The righteous suffer from doubts within and poverty and hardships without. No matter how carefully they obey the law, they cannot escape suffering in some serious form or other. The Psalmist's first impulse was to lift an outraged protest against the way his faith had deceived him in this matter. He seems even to have toyed with the idea of exposing the deception to his children but the thought of doing that, in his own words, "was too painful for me."

Burdened with this struggle, he made his way to the temple, and there, as we might say, the scales fell from his eyes and he received a new perspective on this entire matter. What had looked one way outside the sanctuary was wholly different on the inside.

On the outside, it looked like evil paid—at least it did not come a cropper, as it was supposed to do. Proud, violent, conceited, impious men enjoyed the fruits promised righteous people: prosperity, strength, peace in life and in death. And while the Psalmist was outside the temple, he had to admit that he both envied the wicked their lot and repented of his efforts to live a godly life.

It was a deeply troubled man who entered the temple, stood before the altar, and lifted his heart with his hands to the God of all, seeking light and peace on this matter. His own description of what happened there cannot be improved upon: it was "as a dream when one awaketh"—though "nightmare" might have been a better word. As he awakened, one thing towered above all else: Evil is evil at all times, in all places, and in all people. Evil is evil because it is a violation of the will of God for life. No matter how successful it seems to be in terms of power, wealth or anything else, evil is still evil in the sight of God, and the wise man will accept that grim fact at face value.

The moral order of God will have the last word on the evildoer— and it will be a full answer given in God's own way and time. The evildoer may be prosperous, but he is fated to answer to the One who has asked men to put faithfulness and righteousness ahead of all else. The evildoer may be violent, conceited and powerful, but he is doomed to stand before One the power of whose will is immeasurable—and it will be a day of grim reckoning.

Therefore the Psalmist resolved not to envy the proud, violent, conceited, impious man even though he might sleep well, be prosperous and strong, and die a peaceful death while the Psalmist struggled along the rugged pathway of righteousness.

But the Psalmist does not let himself off with a series of sharp judgments on other evildoers—he knows himself to have been one too. He sees the evil in himself in its true light. He has been a man of feeble faith. He has been tempted to the point of betrayal. He has actually coveted the fruits of unrighteousness and has envied the evildoer. He has all but taken the devious ways of godless men in preference to the straight way of faithfulness to the Lord of Life. This has been his sin, and he seeks forgiveness for it.

I must confess that while the final movement in the Psalmist's experience is human enough to be understood by everyone, it leaves much to be desired—at least, it seems so to all who take seriously the teachings of another Jewish seer many centuries later.

The awakened Psalmist begs forgiveness for the evil that is in him—which is proper—and he calls down the judgment of God on other evildoers with a relish and conviction that stops us short in our tracks. Whereas he cried, "O God, damn them for what they do!" the One who was to come would say, "Father, forgive them, for they know not what they do!"

Jesus would agree with two of the three steps taken by the Psalmist in his approach to evil: First, identify it—evil is evil now and always. Second, grapple with it—renounce it, repel its efforts to conquer you and all others. Then comes the radically different third step. Whereas the Psalmist would say, "Meet evil in others by calling down the wrath of God on them in judgment and punishment," Jesus would say, "Overcome evil with good, by identifying yourself with the evildoer, seeking the redemption of his soul and the transformation of his life by your love and your help."

Look at the miracle that might happen in this and every other sanctuary in the world: We could learn that evil is evil and learn how to address ourselves to it in full seriousness: identify it, grapple with it, and seek to overcome it with good by an identification of ourselves with the evildoer, seeking the redemption of his soul and the transformation of his life. What a different estimate that places upon the worth of religion and upon the Church!

II

If our religion is worth its salt, it ought to help us when and where we most need help—the moment of moral choice, when we

must distinguish between right and wrong, good and evil. It ought
to help identify these moral alternatives, to call them by their
proper name, and to be guided by that fact.

I do not pretend that this is a simple task—an open and shut
case. William James once warned that "in the moment of moral
choice, we have our deepest dealings with the universe." Which is
a way of saying that when we are trying to decide what is right and
wrong, good and evil, we are actually trying to think God's thought
after Him. And it is good Biblical teaching that God is no passive
spectator in this moment of choice. At least the prophets seem to
hear Him saying, "Woe unto you who call evil good and good
evil"; "Cease to do evil, learn to do good." The moral law is God's
continuing word to us about the meaning of our life. And He is
trying to speak to us when we most need to hear it if we will but
listen.

It is true that Christianity does not hand us a code of morality
complete in every detail, but it is likewise true that Christianity is
a flaming faith in One whose will is the moral order of the universe
and who asks that we find our way in His will.

"How," you may ask, "does that help us? On the one hand you
say we are to believe in the reality of a moral order; on the other
you admit we have no specific moral codes on which to base judgments of good and evil, right and wrong. Yet you say if our religion
is worth its salt it will help us make such judgments! Pray tell
how!"

This is a fair challenge—one that must be met. How did the
experience of the Holy in the sanctuary help the Psalmist in his
judgment of good and evil, as obviously it did? So far as I can see
the help came through the realization that so long as there is a
God there is a right and a wrong, and so long as there is a right it
ought to be sought and chosen. His experience of God gave him a
firm foundation for moral judgments. He lived in a world where
evil is evil and good is good. He was given the task of discovering
the difference between the two and abiding by it. Once sure of the
reality of God, he was sure of the necessity of making clear moral

judgments—judgments based on the reality of God, not on the changing currents of human affairs.

Perhaps it is possible to suggest the importance of this experience by comparing two not-so-fictitious situations. In the first, someone says to us, "Let's play a game of looking for something." "Looking for what?" you ask. "Oh, just anything!" "Where shall we look?" "Oh, just anywhere!" "Why look for it at all?" "Oh, it makes us more comfortable to be doing something."

A good many people feel that we are in some such predicament as this when we seek for morality. We can define it as we will, seek for it wherever we choose, and do so simply in order to be able to get along together. This line of reasoning reminds me a little of one of Fitzgerald's descriptions of life: "Life," he said, "is a football game; everyone is off side, and the rules abolished and the referee chased off the field."

In the second situation we are told, "We've lost something—a pen—here in this room and we need it to write letters. Will you help us find it?" We have actually lost something far more important than any one thing: our moral codes have lost their religious foundation, and we need to find it again if they are to have any power or persuasion in life. We know where to look for it—in the sanctuary. We know what it is we are trying to find—a deep personal experience of the reality of God and of His claim on our life. As we find and renew it we will discover with the Psalmist that our religious faith will help us make moral judgments: It will help us realize that evil is evil and good is good; it will help us know the difference between good and evil and to be willing and able to choose the good; it will keep us forever humble about our judgments, knowing that neither they nor we are perfect; it will keep us "learners in the school of life" as long as we live.

Men are building moral codes all of the time—must build them if they are to live together. Some are built on the worship of tradition or of state, or of our way of life. The Christian faith bids us worship the God of the universe and find therein the true foundation of a morality that is universal in its scope and concern. In a world done to death by partisan and provincial moralities aimed to

benefit a few at the expense of the rest, it is high time we sought
and found again one that is interested in the will of God for all
men everywhere.

III

Nor can the Christian Church shrink from her duty in this
crucial task. Yet as she assumes it she will need to change some of
her deeply ingrained habits. She will stop trying to please people
and will take seriously her call to serve God. She will cease trying
to be all things to all people. A Church that tries to be all things
to all people may be an excellent and acceptable social institution,
but she will not be the Church. Let her try to be all things to all
people, and she will find that Phyllis McGinley's little poem, "This
Side of Calvin," [1] describes her perfectly:

> The Reverend Dr. Harcourt, folk agree,
>   Nodding their heads in solid satisfaction,
> Is just the man for this community.
>   Tall, young, urbane, but capable of action,
> He pleases where he serves. He marshals out
>   The younger crowd, lacks trace of clerical unction,
> Cheers the Kiwanis and the Eagle Scout,
>   Is popular at every public function,
>
> And in the pulpit eloquently speaks
>   On divers matters with both wit and clarity:
> Art, Education, God, the Early Greeks,
>   Psychiatry, Saint Paul, true Christian charity,
> Vestry repairs that shortly must begin—
>   All things but Sin. He seldom mentions Sin.

Still another poet, T. S. Eliot, knows that the Church must
speak about sin whether men want to hear it or not. He asks and
answers:

Why should men love the Church? Why should they love her laws?
She tells them of Life and Death, and of all that they would forget.

[1] From *Stories from a Glass House*. Copyright, 1946, by Phyllis McGinley,
originally published in *The New Yorker*. Reprinted by permission of The
Viking Press.

She is tender where they would be hard, and hard where they would
be soft.
She tells them of Evil and Sin, and other unpleasant facts.[2]

The Church—*this* church—must seek to be the Church of God,
the preacher of the Gospel, to all men, but this is far from saying
that she must be all things to all men. She must be *one thing to
all men*. She must seek one thing: to preach the Gospel that in
Christ we have our clearest revelation of the will of God for man.
She must measure all life by that standard. Therefore, she must
both believe in the reality of evil and speak of evil, sin, judgment
and other unpleasant facts. But she will not be content with this—
for her Gospel is positive—she will speak of good, salvation, of the
love of God and of the Kingdom of God.

Men in search of a purpose for life, men aware of the aimless,
patternless, purposeless lives they live from day to day, men sick to
death of the confusion and compromises that blur their vision of
life and duty will welcome the clear witness of the Church no
matter how austere and difficult it may seem. A person who knows
himself to be seriously ill is ready for serious treatment.

The editors of *Fortune* magazine were badly frightened along
with everyone else in 1940 by the chaotic events that were engulf-
ing the world, but they came up with some insights into the true
source of our trouble. They said,

. . . in order for humanity to progress, it . . . must have faith . . .
that absolute spiritual values exist. The Church, as teacher and interpreter of those values, is the guardian of our faith in them. . . . Without spiritual leadership the maladjustments of our politico-economic
system must inevitably increase . . . collectivism will grow; and what
remains to us of the golden age, when we were able to believe [in absolute values], will be consumed in revolutions and wars.

This cry for the Church to be the Church, to become once more
the sanctuary in which men would find God, has come from many
quarters in our disillusioned and desperate world. Mr. Stephen
Spender, one of Britain's outstanding men of letters of our time,

[2] From *The Rock* by T. S. Eliot. Copyright, 1934, by Harcourt, Brace &
Company, Inc. Reprinted by permission of the publisher.

once told why he gave up his genial paganism and smart agnosticism and found his way into the Church:

> I wanted to know the answer of good and evil; what was unbearable
> was to think that there is no moral awakening, that we creep from
> moment to moment deceiving ourselves, sometimes guilty and remorseful, sometimes happy, but never knowing the answer, never seeing
> things as a whole.

Like the Psalmist, Mr. Spender and many another contemporary found the matter too painful for him until he went to the sanctuary—then he knew!

Knew what?

Knew that God alone is the Lord of Life; knew that because of that fact good is good and evil is evil; knew that even as they are different in God's world, they are different and must be distinguished in our life; knew that no matter how sleek, comfortable, prosperous and powerful evildoers may seem to be, they continue to be evildoers whether they are someone else or are ourselves and are not to be envied by one who seeks to find his way in faithfulness and righteousness; knew that a prerequisite of a vigorous morality is a vital religious experience; knew that the normal place for this experience to occur is in the sanctuary where man meets God; knew that this experience puts an end to the easygoing rationalization by which we tend either to blur the distinction between good and evil or to blend them in such fashion that we can no longer tell one from the other.

Having been humbled by the experience of meeting God, of seeing ourselves in the perspective of His will, we are prepared to renew our confession of loyalty to Him and to call good good and evil evil. We are ready then to draw some proper moral inferences for our life and times—still calling good good and evil evil. That is the religious background of our social creeds, our many efforts to cope with the injustices and evils in our common life. We call evil evil and grapple with it. But not in the spirit of Hamlet:

> The times are out of joint—
> O cursed spite! that I was ever born to set it right!

Rather, we say—all unworthily—with another, "To this end was I born, and for this cause came I into the world."

The final movement in Christian ethics is not the identification and rejection of evil: it is the identification of ourselves with the evildoer in an effort to save him. All vital Christianity is finally *vicarious* and *redemptive*, doing all we can do for another that we together may find and serve God.

A number of us were talking to a young Chinese Christian who was on his way back to China after World War I. We asked, "Do you think the Christian faith can ever actually influence China?" He answered, "I do not know about that. But I do know I shall try to make it so!"

Without that faith we can do nothing; with it there is nothing we dare not try to do. It is the faith that overcomes the world.

XI

Lost Signs

~~~~~~

SCRIPTURE LESSON: Psalm 74:1–12 (R.S.V.)

TEXT: We do not see our signs; there is no longer any prophet, and there is none among us who knows how long.

I

WHEN adversity strikes we react as men have done from time immemorial: we want to know why God permits it, why He lets it happen to us, what we have done to deserve such treatment at His hand? During the last war when questions like these were erupting on every side, Dr. Henry Hitt Crane, one of our best-known and loved preachers, addressed himself directly to them in a sermon entitled, "What on earth is God doing?"

The writer of the 74th Psalm was raising much the same question in the second century B.C. Few psalms equal it in vividness; none surpass it as a clear reflection and expression of tragedy in the life of a people. It comes from a day when the ancient Jewish faith in God and man was being strained to the breaking point. It comes from the heart of one who, while believing in God, simply could not understand God's relationship to the evil that was swirling all around him. Our appreciation of the point as well as the poignancy of the Psalm is heightened when we glance at the conditions that produced it. Not that we are utterly unfamiliar with them! In fact, some of them have an ominously contemporary ring.

For two hundred years before the Psalm was written Palestine had been under the political rule of, first, the Persian, then the

Greek empires. Although restless under foreign domination, the Jews were unable to throw it off and had finally given up trying. The ruling powers permitted them to rebuild their temple in Jerusalem, to build synagogues in outlying towns, and, in general, to retain ancestral ways in worship and faith. Although under Greek rule, they lived, thought and worshiped as Jews. But, with the death of Alexander the Great, all this changed. Civil war broke out among the pieces of his empire, and, as usual, little Palestine was caught in the pincers of power politics.

One of the rulers, Antiochus Epiphanes, determined to break down the separatism of the Jews and make them real members of the Greek states. He wanted no dissatisfied minorities in his kingdom. Realizing that they would put up vigorous resistance, and knowing that their religion would be the heart of their resistance, he struck directly and boldly at the synagogues and the Temple. He burned the synagogues throughout the land; he desecrated the Temple in every conceivable way. The sacred altar was torn down and a Greek one set up; the great wooden trellises that separated the altar from the court were literally chopped to pieces; every religious emblem or sign in the Temple was torn down and symbols of Greek faith, culture and power put in their place; loud revelry replaced the quiet solemnity of the ancient Hebrew Temple rites.

This is what the Psalmist saw and heard when he went to the Temple:

> Thy foes have roared in the midst of thy holy place;
>> they set up their own signs for signs.
> At the upper entrance they hacked
>> the wooden trellis with axes.
> And then all its carved wood
>> they broke down with hatchets and hammers.
> They set thy sanctuary on fire;
>> to the ground they desecrated the dwelling place of
>> thy name.
> They said to themselves, "We will utterly subdue them";
>> they burned all the meeting places of God in the land.

> We do not see our signs;
>> there is no longer any prophet,
>> and there is none among us who knows how long.

Then, doubt and bitterness well up from this horror and help-lessness at what he sees and frame these questions:

> How long, O God, is the foe to scoff?
>> Is the enemy to revile thy name for ever?
> Why dost thou hold back thy hand,
>> why dost thou keep thy right hand in thy bosom?

For a moment the Psalmist, like so many of us when in adver-sity, is in danger of succumbing to the lure of pessimism and cyni-cism: no signs, no prophet, no hope—almost no God! But he catches himself on the very edge of that moral and spiritual preci-pice! One more step or slip would have been fatal. Had he taken it, he would have forsaken his ancestral faith and thrown in his lot with the Greek oppressors, reasoning, "Might makes right," or "God is on the side of the biggest battalions." Some of his con-temporaries did just that, but not many. Most Jews, like the Psalm-ist, were more than thoroughly dismayed by the disasters that had overtaken them; they were driven back to what one of our poets, Marie Santos, has called "the deep sources" of their faith. "Yet God my king is from old, working salvation in the midst of the earth." With this renewal of their faith in God and His purpose in the world, they were ready for the fight to a finish with their tormentors—a fight which they fought and won.

Though the conquerors might burn the Law, deface and dese-crate the altar, and remove hallowed symbols of faith from the Temple, neither their hands nor their hatchets nor their swords could reach the faith that had created the symbols, written the Law and built the Temple. So long as that faith lived and was regnant in their hearts, the symbols could be replaced, the Law rewritten and the Temple rebuilt.

Though we have tried many other ways over the intervening centuries, we have found no better way to cope with the threat of cynicism and pessimism than to return to the deep sources of faith in the Hebrew-Christian tradition. And as we do this we shall find signs and symbols of the reality, the purpose and the love of God, as well as of his expectations of us, that quite meet every need. These signs that man can neither give nor take away yield confidence in the will of God even in dark days and the courage to continue to trust in Him when evils threaten to overwhelm life and faith alike.

Is there a person here who will not confess to himself that he has needed, now needs and will need all his life this confidence in God which is fundamental to confidence in life and strength for living?

"But needing it and getting it honestly are two quite different things," you say. "What do you mean by 'the deep sources of our faith?' " you want to know. In answer, I should like to direct your attention to the three great words or symbols of the will of God for the life of man that have stood the test of time. These, I am convinced, suggest the difference between despair and hope, cynicism and trust, pessimism and confidence. Our fathers before us found this to be true, and common sense as well as our common need require us to look at them with some care.

II

We see, first, the Decalogue, the Ten Commandments. They are first in point of time and almost in point of influence on our tradition. Although many of these commandments were not original with the Hebrews, no other people made so original a use of them as did the Hebrews. The Decalogue became the basis of the thought and life of that people. They were the moral foundations on which the Hebrews tried to build their nation and their entire culture.

That is why they loom so large in the Old Testament. They were not laws to be engraved on tables of stone and erected in prominent places in the Temple and regarded as signs of piety; they were vital commandments from God to be written on the hearts of the faithful, and used as guides for living.

Fathers and mothers were asked to teach them to their children

from earliest infancy. Rabbis spent a lifetime searching out the
fuller meaning and application of them. Temple and synagogue
centered their life in them. That is why we call the Decalogue
fundamental to the Hebrews.

More than that, they are fundamental to any enduring society
and civilization. We have outgrown many things which seemed
important to the early Hebrews but not these: Reverence for God;
serious and sustained worship of God; respect for person, rights
and property. These are as basic as ever. No person or society is
going to get far either in their absence or in defiance of them.

The *Reader's Digest* recently carried a story which illustrates the
indestructibility of the Ten Commandments. Morning after morning a minister passed a huge construction job on the highway, and
each time he noticed a man pounding away with a sledge at a pile
of big rocks that he was breaking up. One morning the minister
said to him, "That pile of rocks doesn't go down very fast, does it?"
The worker paused before replying, "No sir, they don't! They are
something like the Ten Commandments—you can break them up
into little pieces, but they are still here." Which calls to mind one
of the truest and most famous things ever said by A. Maude Roy-
den, "You can't break the Ten Commandments, but you can break
yourself against them."

Stories about Mark Twain keep cropping up on all matters. One
that I like best tells of the hypocritical old business pirate who told
him, "Before I die I mean to make a pilgrimage to the Holy Land.
I want to climb to the top of Mount Sinai and read the Ten Commandments aloud." "I have a better idea," suggested Mark Twain.
"Why don't you stay right at home in Boston and keep them?"

III

It must have been solid comfort to the Psalmist as he walked
away from the disheartening destruction of holy things to refresh
his spirit at still another deep source of his faith where he found
something so true, so deeply spiritual that it, too, was beyond the
profaning power of the conqueror.

> He has showed you, O man, what is good;
> and what does the Lord require of you

but to do justice, and to love kindness,
and to walk humbly with your God?

Repeating these immortal words to himself, he took courage.
For the true signs and symbols of great faith are not altars,
temples, synagogues and sacred scrolls, precious as these are; they
are a quality of life and a certain way of living.

Strangely enough, when Micah was framing this one insight that
is better known than any other part of his book, he was not lament-
ing the strokes of adversity, he was warning against the seductions
of prosperity. When Micah visited the Temple it was crowded
with Hebrews; their signs and symbols were seen on every hand;
priests were at the altar; ancestral rites were being performed; no
enemy was at hand or even in sight, so far as they knew. Micah
was disturbed at the ease with which religion became a matter of
ritual and propriety. He believed that it had become so institu-
tionalized that people were forgetting the deeper spiritual concerns
of humility, justice and kindness.

Here, then, were two men separated by five hundred years and
facing quite different scenes in the Temple, coming to the same
general conclusion: the true symbols of religion are spiritual and
ethical ideals and behavior. Important as institutions may be in the
nurture of such ideals, they must never get between men and those
ideals. Living as we do in a time when churches generally are pros-
pering, when the measure of greatness in a church is usually the
size and beauty of a building, we need to read in humility the lines
of Nancy Byrd Turner as she studied the beautiful cathedral of St.
John the Divine in New York City:

> Good Saint, they've housed you now in costly stone,
> Great soaring arch and plinth and polished rock—
> You who in exile, beggared and alone,
> Reported Heaven itself from one bare rock.[1]

When we get to talking too much about the Church and too
little about God, too much about the Church and too little about
Jesus Christ, too much about theology and too little about personal

[1] *Atlantic Monthly*, August, 1934.

relations, too much about attending services and too little about periods of personal worship, let us turn again to Micah and the Psalmist and let them help us get things in proper perspective again.

IV

Nearly two hundred years after the Psalmist lived, the wheel of fortune had taken another turn, for the Jews and their beloved Temple had been both restored and enlarged under the leadership of Herod the Great. In fact, it was so impressively beautiful that one of the proverbs of the period said, "Say not you have seen a thing of beauty until you have seen Herod's Temple." The Jews were proud of it and gloried in the privilege of worshiping in it. For ever so many of them it symbolized God's full will for them. They called it "the dwelling place of the Most High." Going to the Temple; taking the correct offering to the Temple; facing toward the Temple when they prayed—slowly, surely and understandably the Temple became a if not the central symbol of religious faith for them.

But not for all. As a young teacher and his followers were leaving the Temple one day, one of them exclaimed over the beauty and majesty of it. Jesus answered almost casually that the Temple could be destroyed again as it had been several times before. Then, like Micah and the Psalmist, he tried to get his hearers to pay attention to the signs of true religion. In the midst of the give-and-take of one such discussion, he was challenged to summarize the vast heritage of Hebrew law. Who can forget his answer? "You shall love the Lord your God with all your heart, with all your soul, with all your mind, with all your strength; and your neighbor as yourself."

Here, as we well know, is one of the deep sources of the Christian faith—one to which Jesus tried to get his hearers to return when hypnotized by the grandeur of the Temple, or lulled into ethical complacency by the magnificent ritual of the Temple, or filled with self-righteousness because they had obeyed to the letter a hundred little laws governing speech, dress and deportment.

Abraham Lincoln once observed that he would gladly join any church that had as its creed Jesus' summary of the Law. Not many of us, I think, would want to argue with Lincoln on that point. The very existence of Jesus' statement has posed a question of conscience for all churchmen from that day to our own. While they have hoped—as we continue to hope—that our beautiful churches, our precise theologies and our stately ritual will actually help one to the point where he will love God and man utterly, we can only confess that all too frequently this does not happen. Men have been content with these symbols of the Christian life; they have not pushed on to the deep sources of that life in all-consuming love for God and man.

Later in his ministry Jesus spelled out the thing that was to be distinctive about his disciples: "By this shall all men know that you are my disciples, that you love one another." Look at that; then if you can bear the sight, look at the history of the Christian Church and the behavior of Christian people today! Who of us can so much as lift up our eyes before praying, "We have left undone those things we ought to have done and have done those things which we ought not to have done. God be merciful to me a sinner."

V

What would it mean to have—we had better ask what might we expect if we were to have—a generation nourishing their spirits at the deep sources of our religious heritage? No one can hope to give a complete answer to that, of course, but we may be sure that certain things would happen.

For one thing, we would recover the spiritual foundations of our faith and life. We of the twentieth century would know that the true glory of our faith is to be found where Micah, the Psalmist, and Jesus of Nazareth said it was: in a sincere personal relationship of love for, and trust in, God. We would know that He is not far from us no matter what is happening. We would face the problems of our own life and the broad ones of our time with the same trust that caused the Psalmist to cry, "Yet God my king is of old, working salvation in the midst of the earth." That would be our answer to those who wonder what on earth God is doing—He is "working salvation" in our very midst! Even when we cannot discover the precise ways in which He is working we would not collapse into cynicism and despair, saying either that He does not exist or that He does not care. We should know that He does exist, that He does care, and that as we live and work in patience and trust, we shall be able to discern His saving work in our very midst.

There is needful humility, peace of soul and steady power for living in this attitude toward life. If it is to mean anything at all at some one time—say, in difficult days—then we should make its cultivation one of our major concerns all of the time. Don't, I beg of you, don't wait for "the fell clutch of circumstance" to enfold you before you start building your life on the firm foundation of faith in God! I find it next to impossible to communicate an awareness of, and confident trust in, God to those who never give Him so much as a passing thought until they are in direst need. Not being accustomed to face life with and in Him and His purpose, it is hard for them to live and walk by faith as one must when blinded by sorrow and tragedy.

We sang—and how we sang!—"God Bless America" when we faced the ordeal of World War II. One member of the church I was serving at the time asked that we sing it before the benediction at the conclusion of the services of worship each Sunday! I might have been friendlier to the notion if it had come up in time of prosperity and peace. I was and am of the opinion that we have many hymns in the hymnal that do more justice to God's purpose for all men than that particular one. Kipling's "Recessional," though embalmed in a practically unsingable tune, impresses me as one such. Nations, like men, at the height of their power and prosperity are usually blinded by pride even as they are blinded by fear when in the depths of bitter struggle—and religious faith must minister with even hand to both periods, trying to persuade men to be humbly aware of Him in all things.

A second result of returning to the deep sources of our faith will be an outgrowth of the first: We will reject all pagan substitutes for them.

The early Church rejected emperor worship even though in so doing she brought down on her head the wrath of the Roman Empire. Twenty years ago, the German churches rejected Alfred Rosenberg's Nordic Cult and touched off a conflict with the government of the Third Reich that never ceased. The Russian Church has steadily and openly rejected the materialistic defamation of life that is fundamental to orthodox Communist thought, and there is not the slightest reason to think she will ever accept or even tolerate it. While she will not lead an armed crusade to overthrow it, she is waging her own kind of war with it. Each time a priest goes to the altar to celebrate the Mass, each time the faithful gather to sing the great hymns of the Church—and the delegation of British Quakers who visited Russia some time ago tell of overflowing churches—each time, I say, these things happen, the Church is both rejecting a pagan substitute and bearing her witness to the fact that God is "working salvation in the midst of the earth."

Let us for our part as Christian churchmen of our own beloved country mount vigilant guard against similar pagan substitutes. Secularism is our great foe, and we meet it in force wherever we turn. Secularism exalts man and either rejects or ignores God. Secularism holds that "we are the masters of our fate," that this is "the American Century," that "how we use our wealth and power is strictly our own affair."

Many of us are more than a little concerned about the deep inroads secularism has made in our schools. Wherever this has happened we find a neglect of religious and moral values in the curriculum and general school program. This we think is a serious mistake. An education without an awareness of such values may be a thorough preparation for a job, but it is a poor preparation for life. As recently as a century ago, secularism was practically unknown in our schools. At that time the unifying purpose of the schools was clearly understood and accepted by schoolmen and community alike. "It was to train the Christian citizen." The secularist influence has made us all too content merely to train people for jobs, and we are becoming progressively the poorer for it in every way.

That, I am sure, is what prompted James B. Conant, former president of Harvard University, to appoint a commission to study the objectives of a general education. He said that an education must be regarded as incomplete if it did not teach the student that "right and wrong" are ethical as well as mathematical terms! Fortunately, the National Education Association agrees with him and has published a remarkable study of the place of moral and spiritual values in the schools. This, I should like to believe, is the good sense of the American people in returning to the deep sources of our faith in God as the foundation of life. However much we may sin against it—and we do—we are not wholly lost so long as we return to it and see life in its perspective.

The second pagan substitute for great faith that we must spot and reject is the jingo patriotism that is always candidating for our spirits, especially in periods of tension. The best example of it I have yet found appeared in the magazine section of the *Baltimore Sun* in January, 1942, just as we were entering the war. Under the heading, "We Have a Date with Destiny," there occurred these remarkable words:

We're the best, the biggest. We've got everything. We're the tops. We've got pride, strength, courage. This—1942—is going to be our year. We know it. We can't miss. Nobody's going to push the U. S. A. around. That's why we're the tops. That's why we're going to keep on being the tops. . . . We're not boasting. But we're strong and proud and confident. We have reason to be. We know we've got it—the best of everything. We know that we'll keep it. You can't beat us. We're David and Goliath both. Let some of those tough boys figure out a way to beat that combination.

I remember reading and rereading it, scarcely able to believe that I was reading it. Then I laid the paper down with the strong feeling that if that was our date with destiny it was a blind date undertaken for strictly immoral purposes!

Sometimes in my gloomier moments, I seem to hear America

trying to pray. Standing erect with face lifted toward God, this is what she says: "Dear God, we are grateful for everything that we have in life. We have built here a powerful civilization. We have built the most efficient industrial order ever known to man. We have shared in the discovery of the secrets of the basic energy of the universe itself. We have used it to make the most powerful weapons of war ever devised by man. . . ."

And, at this point, God interrupts to ask, "Yes, I know, but have you learned to love one another? Remember? That is what I asked you to do?"

Then, the face of America pales; she drops to her knees and with bowed head prays, "God be merciful to me a sinner!"

Let this generation nourish its spirit on the deep sources of our faith that God is working His salvation in our midst, and we will be able to keep love of country from assuming dangerous forms. We as a people will be called to repentance before God for the evils in our life and ways. We as a people will be humbled by our unfitness to bear witness to our faith in Him, but we will bear it nonetheless. We as a people will be determined to build here a country whose motto will be "In God we trust." And our only chance to succeed is to make sure that motto is inscribed on our hearts and in our behavior rather than simply on our coins.

Hartley Coleridge, little-known son of the famous Samuel Taylor Coleridge, posed this searching question in one of his poems:

> In holy books we read how God hath spoken
> To holy men in many different ways;
> But hath the present world no sign or token?
> Is God quite silent in these latter days?

The answer, of course, is and must always be "No!" The present world does have signs and tokens of the will of God working salvation in our very midst. He is no more silent now than at any other time in human life and history. If we do not hear Him, it may be because we are not listening for Him. If we do not see Him, it may be because we are looking for something else. If we do not feel

Him, it is high time we drop everything else as of secondary importance and make our way to the deep source of our faith.

When the late Dean Willard L. Sperry said that it is the task of the Church to make God real to every generation, he was giving us our marching orders. That is our date with destiny as a Church. Let us not fail to keep it—for the preservation and perpetuation of all that we hold dear hinges upon it.

XII

My God and King!

~~~~~~

SCRIPTURE LESSON: Psalm 74:1–23

TEXT: For God is my King of old, working salvation in the midst of
the earth.

I

THE 74th Psalm speaks with startling directness to what has been
called "The Predicament of Modern Man." There is, I should
suppose, no secret about the fact that we are in a predicament of
some sort or other, and that it is a serious one. There seems to be
a great deal of honest disagreement about the reason or reasons for
the predicament. There are many different suggestions as to how
to get out of it.

It might be well, at the very outset, to get a clearer notion of
what constitutes a predicament. I think of one very human illustration. A boy came to his father with this not unfamiliar word,
"Dad, I'd like to have the car this Saturday night. I've got to have
it because I've already got a date and I've told my girl that I would
have the car." The father thought a moment before replying,
"Well, that's too bad. I've already made plans to use the car myself
that night." The boy exclaimed, "Say, Dad! this *is* a predicament!"

Moving a little closer to an exact statement: when you are in a
situation where you must do something, yet do not know what to
do, and time is running out on you—you are in a predicament, and
you know the predicament we are in today. When you feel called
upon to proclaim a belief or set of beliefs about God, Man and
History that are not shared in any serious way by your contem-

poraries who will almost certainly misunderstand you—you are both in a predicament and you share the predicament of the confessing Christian today. When you feel compelled by loyalty to these convictions to initiate or to support a course of action in the life of a people who do not share these convictions and, therefore, cannot be expected either to understand or support your proposals —you are both in a predicament and you are in the permanent predicament of the convinced Christian.

Actually, the predicament we face today could be described in some such pedestrian way as this: We have tried to get along without the discipline, guidance and power of great religion in human life and affairs only to discover matters going from bad to worse in many fundamental ways. Edwin Arlington Robinson, one of our most discerning contemporaries, puts it in his own poetic way, "The world is a spiritual kindergarten where a lot of bewildered children are trying to spell out 'God' with the wrong blocks."

Much of the pathos of our predicament grows out of our reluctance to face the fact that this is the real nature of our trouble. While I should like to go along with the current cliché, born more of fear than of fact, that "we are essentially religious people," I'm afraid one of our educators is nearer the truth about us when he writes, "America is not religiously minded, however religiously starved it may be." There is no reason to limit such starvation to America. If we are so starved, and I think we are, so is the rest of the world. That makes the predicament all the worse. Where then can we turn—or is there anywhere to turn—for a new go at this business of living?

Even as we object to the extreme nature of the charge that we are spiritually "starved," we cannot shrug off Dr. Elton Trueblood's insistence that we do not have the depth of faith we need in order to cope with the problems we face. Living as we are in a day when the battle of the ultimates is on all through life, many of us not only do not know which side we are on, but we also are not sure where the real battle line is. We have been coasting along with the momentum of our fathers' faith but with little or no clearly held and deeply committed faith of our own. This seems to

work out so long as the road slopes gently downhill, but when we
face steep problems and need power for acceleration, we are in a
predicament. And that is the situation that many of us find ourselves in as we face our personal as well as social problems.

II

As I stated at the beginning, the writer of the 74th Psalm speaks
as a contemporary. If we are able to take his experience and advice
with any degree of seriousness, they may provide us, as they have
others before us, with precisely the pivot we need in order to find
the right direction out of the spiritual predicament of our time.

The Psalm consists of twenty-three verses and falls into two
general lines of thought, with the twelfth verse serving as the pivot
on which we swing from one line of thought to the other. The
first half of the Psalm details the tragedy and woe that had befallen
Israel, Jerusalem and the Temple. The writer's faith dims down
and almost flickers out as he contemplates all this. Then comes
the pivot of his thought: "For God is my King of old, working
salvation in the midst of the earth." And, swinging round this
affirmation, his faith looks up again and gains strength steadily
throughout the remainder of the Psalm. He celebrates God as the
Creator of the Universe, the Lord of all life, and the Redeemer of
Israel. Still vividly aware of the seriousness of the situation which
surrounds him, he nonetheless faces it now with confident hope
and aggressive courage. He has found the peace of mind that
comes with great convictions and the power for living that comes
from committing oneself to them. He had found a way out of his
spiritual predicament; he was ready for a fresh go at the cumulative
tragedy of his day.

I want to draw the obvious conclusion that, in the judgment of
historic religion, the pivot we need and the only one capable of
swinging us out of our predicament and giving us a fresh go at life
is indicated by the faith that enables a man to say "My God and
King" as he faces the problems of his life and time. And, in addition, I want to underscore the conviction that it is high time we
stopped making what Emerson once scathingly called "polite bows

to God" and started taking seriously the simple fact that belief in God and commitment to God rank at the very top of the basic needs of this generation of bedeviled men and beleaguered civilizations.

I am quite prepared for the storm that this insistence will encounter from many of our contemporaries who have long since written religion off as fit for the museum rather than the market place. "Stop right there," they say. "Do you mean that we've got to get back to a belief that we discarded long ago in order to find a way out of the mess we are in today?"

I mean just that. If we are serious about the effort to get out of the situation in which we find ourselves, we shall have to lay hold on a faith in God that both persuades our mind and controls our life. So far from being irrelevant to the great issues of our life and time, this effort takes us to the very heart of them.

The matter might be put this way: When the lights go out in our room, we know that the fault lies in the bulb, the fuse, or the power house. We step into the next room to see if the lights are on there. If they are out there, we conclude that a fuse has gone out, but before tinkering with that we take a look at the neighbors' houses to see if their lights are burning. If they too dwell in darkness, we conclude that the trouble probably is not local at all but is to be located in the powerhouse. We know that when it is fixed there we shall have light once more.

After making due allowance for the weakness of any such mechanical illustration, it does point up the relationship of the idea of God to our ordinary life. It is the powerhouse that governs the light of ethical codes and standards of value that we use consciously or not all through our life. And when the lights go out —as they seem now to have gone out—of the basic moral codes of mankind, we had better pay some attention to the spiritual powerhouse which makes them radiant with meaning.

III

When we say and believe "My God and King," we are doing just that. This affirmation is no vague, fearful, emotionalized flight from the problems men must face. It is a thoroughly alert and responsible way of thinking about the world. Yes, "thinking" was the word I used. Not "wishing and hoping," but "thinking"—hard-bitten, realistic thinking about the way in which known facts fit into a kind of frame of universal meaning. To say, as great religion always has and always will, "I believe in God as the Creator of the Universe, the Lord of Life and the One in whom we live and move and have our being" is not to be out of step with the most powerful currents in contemporary scientific, philosophical and religious thought. Rather, it is little more than a fair summary of what has been happening in these great disciplines of the human mind. Look, for just a moment, at what I mean.

Science tells a story which though incomplete in detail is precise in outline and meaning. Sir Arthur Eddington once described the vocation of the scientist this way: "There's something going on in this universe and it's our business to find out what it is." Well, modern science has done a speedy and remarkably convincing job of providing the factual outline of the nature of this world. All the risks of oversimplification must be run in order to grasp the probing realism and factual content of the affirmation, "I believe in God."

For in this world, the ultimate unit of existence, whether energy or matter or both, is what it is by virtue of its interrelationships. Nothing stands alone in this universe. Electrons and protons, and God alone knows what else, unite to form atoms; atoms to form molecules; molecules cells, cells tissues; tissues organs, organs organisms. Then the social sciences take up the story and tell how organisms unite to produce societies of one sort or another—some simple, others incredibly complex. Once man could do his thinking in terms of family and tribe; now he must do it in terms of civilizations and the human family.

Philosophers from Socrates to Whitehead have suspected that something like this was going on and have built imposing systems of thought to interpret the fuller meaning of it for the life of man. Man does not live unto himself alone. He, too, is a part not only of the social stream, but of the entire universe itself. He gets his life from others; his life has no meaning unless he can share it with others; the greatest tragedy that can befall him is to be separated from those relationships that give life meaning. Whatever else the good or the abundant life may mean, it will include a conscious and responsible relationship of man with man and with God. The Christian faith, accustomed to having its ideals of love and brotherhood derided by worldlings as unrealistic and fanciful, now can hardly believe its ears when it hears them acknowledging that they are not only intellectually respectable but actually confront the world with our only alternative to growing disorder and final disaster. We are either going to work for the Kingdom of God here and now or we shall surely witness the end of the kingdoms of man here and now.

The scientist in his laboratory, the philosopher in his study, and the Christian as he works with the breaking minds and spirits of our time, all know this to be true. They know, too, that if there is any alternative to futility and disaster it lies somewhere in the affirmation, "My God and King."

IV

In addition to being an alert and respectable way of thinking about the world, "My God and King" is an alert and responsible way of living in this world.

It is a way of life that gives up once and for all the sophomoric delusions of grandeur that

> I am the master of my fate;
> I am the Captain of my soul,

and accepts at face value the simple fact that life as we know it is both a gift from God and a precious possession that we share with others. Knowing this to be the truth about us, we propose to live life in a thoroughly responsible way, to find its deepest meaning by losing it in the great issues of the day rather than fritter it away by humoring our whims and fleeting desires. To this end, then, we solemnly propose to try to find our way in the will of the God of the universe when we say "My God and King." It becomes more, much more, than a simple intellectual belief about the nature of the world; it becomes a proclamation of what the world is trying to do through us. A friend of mine once said, "The miracle of each day is that the God of the Universe can use even me." That is true: indeed, I would say that it is the most glorious truth about human life. It is glory if you accept it and it is tragedy if you don't. For if there be not a meaning in this universe in terms of which you can find the meaning of your own life, the certainty cannot long be put off that your life has no meaning. Then the whole business becomes a snare and a delusion, or as a cynic once put it, "Life is a comedy perfectly re-enacted."

Great religion does not believe that for one moment. For good and sufficient and publicly respectable reasons it insists that

> . . . This world's no blot for us,
> Nor blank—it means intensely and means good:
> To find its meaning is my meat and drink.

Having found the outline of this meaning as a belief that can be held with a free and sincere mind, then we take the next step and accept it as the way of life we propose to follow. If we believe that the God of the Universe is trying to create the great community out of our separate communities, if we believe that He is trying to make his Kingdom out of our kingdoms; if we believe that our clearest revelation of His way of doing this is to be found in the life and teachings of Jesus Christ, our job is cut out for us if we try to find our way in His will.

V

When we say "My God and King" and say it with the full dimension of seriousness that is in it, several results can be guaranteed:

1. We shall find that our own life has new peace and power. Have you been reading the series of articles by Edward R. Murrow entitled "This I Believe"? I am thinking especially of the one written by Justice William O. Douglas of the Supreme Court. He tells of his inability to appreciate something his devout father said

as he approached an operation that might well result in death. "If I die it will be glory; if I live it will be grace." As the years with their weight of care and trouble flew by, it became easier for him to see that his father had hold of something of tremendous importance—something to which he himself is now returning.

2. We shall swing forever away from the worship of the half-gods of State and Our Way of Life and find our purpose in a deathless devotion to the One God—the Creator, Sustainer and Redeemer of the world. Think what that would mean today if six hundred million nominal Christians would take it seriously. For, as Canon F. R. Barry once said, "If God is King, then there is a law higher than any national sovereign state, and to it the Nation must conform or perish. . . . If God is King, then the common man is of infinite worth and preciousness in his sight, and the whole organization of society must be a means to personal fulfillment." Yet, until people like us are willing to say "My God and King" to God and only God, states, nations and ways of life will rise up and command us to fall down and worship them. A new day will dawn when we worship the One God and seek to serve Him alone. That is the Christian answer to statism, communism and every other social and political "ism" known to man.

3. We shall cease letting someone else bear our share of responsibility in building a better world than we have ever had before. We shall rise to the full stature of our manhood under God and seek to be fit embodiments of His holy will for human life. We shall find our way into the fellowship of those who seek to live their life as He wills and we will be responsible, creative members of that fellowship. And we shall do this with the full realization that we shall probably find out in our own experience just why the central symbol of the Christian faith is and will always be—the Cross.

XIII

When Faith Falters[1]

SCRIPTURE LESSON: Psalm 77:1–15

TEXT: Will the Lord cast off forever?
Is his lovingkindness clean gone forever?
Hath God forgotten to be gracious?

I

IN ONE of his books Thornton Wilder tells of an aged missionary bishop who was spending the last two years of his life in retirement in France. The pathos of those years is summed up in this line: "His was a fighting faith, and when he no longer had battles to fight, his faith withered away." I mention this because it suggests the fact we shall be studying this morning: a vital faith is always a fighting faith.

When someone tells me that he has never had a moment of probing religious doubt I find myself wondering whether he has ever known a moment of vital religious conviction. For if one fact stands out above all others in the history of religion, it is this: the price of a great faith is a great and continuous struggle to get it, to keep it and to share it. I know of no exception to this rule among those whose religious faith has changed the course of history. That is why it is a serious mistake to think of faith as a placid lake under the bewitching beauty of the full moon. It is much more like the ocean in storm, the swift current of the full river where one must stay alert if he would stay alive. Faith is a fight as well as peace.

[1] This sermon was preached at the baccalaureate service of Garrett Biblical Institute on June 14, 1953.

Faith is a conflict as well as a peaceful comradeship with God. Faith is a purpose making headway against a storm, adjusting itself to the swiftly rushing current of life and events. These truths about faith we should proclaim to a world that is reaching for every self-advertised brand of it that comes in capsule form. The cost of faith is high, but no higher than we should expect it to be when we consider what it means to us.

Those who want a placid faith in seven easy lessons will want to stay clear of the 77th Psalm. For it is one of our most vivid pictures of a devout man fighting to steady a faltering faith. It can teach us so much about the meaning of faith that it deserves a close look.

The Psalm was written by a pious Jew who lived during the Exile. The hurricane of history had swept over Israel, leveling her entire life and surrounding the survivors with a vast spiritual devastation of her fondest hopes. As the Psalmist surveyed this wreckage he could see no hope of an early end of the tragedy of his people. In fact, he was not at all sure there ever would be an end—and as he struggled with this possibility his faith faltered, and he found himself asking three questions:

1. Will the Lord cast off forever?
   And will He be favorable no more?
2. In His loving-kindness clean gone forever?
   Doth His promise fail forever more?
3. Hath God forgotten to be gracious?
   Hath He in anger shut up His tender mercies?

These are the honest questions of a devout man who is trying to understand the meaning of what is happening. He is no superficial skeptic tossing off flip questions about God and evil. His questions are fair and desperately honest. They come from the heart of a great faith and are forced up to the level of expression by a suffering which ran beyond the bounds of reason and understanding. He simply wants to know whether God has cast off him and his people forever, whether their ancestral faith in God had been mistaken.

The Psalmist is not alone in raising these questions. Prophets before and after him raised them over and over again. Faith—even the faith of great souls—can and does falter upon occasion, and for a number of reasons.

II

The first and most common reason why faith falters is the one we see in the experience of the Psalmist: the occurrence of some tragic event that contradicts or challenges the promises of faith.

Paul's ancestral faith faltered before the steady witness of the early Christians, particularly the stoning of Stephen. He was forced to rethink it, and it simply did not stand up under the ordeal. The early Church was puzzled by the crucifixion of Christ. For half a century after this had happened it looked like a defeat, and Christians were forced to do some of their steadiest thinking about it in order to fit it into the pattern of Christian victory.

In our own lives, the death of a loved one or the defeat of our nation or cause can force our faith to falter. All such events raise doubts about the accuracy of traditional beliefs in the love and the goodness of God. I think it safe to say that faith is faltering all over the world today because of the tragic and unpredictable character of events.

Gabriel Marcel, French philosopher and dramatist, put a play on the French stage a few years ago that contains an eloquent description of our world. One agent cries, "Don't you feel sometimes that we are living . . . in a broken world? Yes, broken like a broken watch. The mainspring has stopped working. Just to look at it, nothing has changed. Everything is in place. But put the watch to your ear, and you don't hear any ticking. You know what I'm talking about: the world, what we call the world of human creatures . . . it seems to me it must have had a heart at one time, but today you would say the heart has stopped beating."

Wherever we turn in a breaking and broken world we find faith faltering and asking, "Hath God forgotten to be gracious? Is His loving-kindness clean gone forever? Will He be favorable no more?"

A second reason why faith falters is the discovery that traditional religious ideas no longer fit our new experiences. This, I should suppose, has happened to everyone in some form or other. And it does not happen once; it will happen many times. The very nature of life makes it almost inescapable. John Dewey based his philosophy on the simple fact that "all action is an invasion of the future, the unknown. Conflict and uncertainty are ultimate traits."

How true we find this to be in the simple process of growing up! There is no way we can begin life with so adequate a system of ideas that our experience does not change them. The wisdom of our parents, while helpful, is not infallible. It can steady us, but it cannot remove the elements of conflict and uncertainty from our life. Yet it is a jar when first we discover their inadequacy, discover that our parents are far from infallible and that we must make our own decisions and find our own way into the future.

One of the reasons why a college campus is such a fascinating place to live and work is the fact that it is the scene of these struggles toward greater maturity on the part of every generation of students. This is no easy road to travel, as all know who have traveled it. All along the way one finds his faith in traditional ideas faltering, finds that he must do some serious thinking for himself if he is to have a vital faith in himself, in his fellow men, in God.

This is no new experience for our religious tradition. Two of the great heroes of early Christianity, Paul and Origen, went through the twilight period of faltering doubt on their way to a greater faith for themselves and for those who were to come after them. Each had been born and nurtured in one tradition and had found that that tradition was seriously challenged by the new Christian faith. It could not have been an easy struggle for them to modify the old and accept the new, but both did it.

Wherever we turn, then, in this matter of living, we find there is some evidence for the generalization that the heresy of yesterday is likely to be the orthodoxy of today and the outmoded good of tomorrow. This progression does not proceed smoothly, like an escalator. It goes by fits and starts, with doubt and faltering faith in evidence all along the way, especially at points of greatest growth. Time and again we will be driven to the mood that prompted Theodore Dreiser to write his poem.[2]

2 "Little Keys." Reprinted by permission of Mrs. Theodore Dreiser.

Little keys
Little keys
That unlock the little doors
To little visions
Little delights—
That open them
To little pleasures
And little pains
That divine so little
Reveal so little
And yet here—
Beyond,
The Great doors
And the great locks;
The giant doors
And the giant locks
That the little keys
Will not unlock.

III

When faith falters, what do we do? What can we do?

Although our first and strongest temptation is to retreat from the challenge to an earlier and stronger position, we have no real alternative to moving steadily ahead through the clouds of lowering doubt, suffering and hardship in search of an even greater faith than we have ever known. Paul could have bowed off the stage of history when he lost faith in Judaism. He could have returned to Tarsus and spent his life making tents and staying well within the limits of traditional thoughts and ways. Had he done so, we would have lost our best example of the sheer power of faith in God. Martin Luther could have done any one of a number of things to relieve the tension of his doubt and suffering, but he chose to move steadily ahead into the thick of battle, both needing and finding an even greater faith in God than he had ever known. The only answer then to a faltering faith is to steady it by advancing through the doubts that challenge it to an even greater faith.

It will be easier for us to gird up our energies for this move ahead if we recall for a moment our indebtedness to those experiences when faith faltered.

We owe the book of Job to a series of men over several generations whose faith in the providence of God faltered in the presence of evil in the world. We owe most of the Old Testament to men whose faith faltered not once, but many times, as they experienced or recalled the tragedies and defeats in Hebrew history. We owe the New Testament to men whose faith in ancestral ideas faltered before the challenge of Christian ideas and experiences. We owe the Reformation to men whose faith under severe challenge pushed beyond the inadequate systems of thought and institutions in which they had been reared to more adequate ones that they passed on to us.

Tennyson's best-known poem, "In Memoriam," grew out of the challenge his faith had to face in the death of a gifted young friend, Arthur Henry Hallam. Hallam died in 1833, and Tennyson brooded over the meaning of the loss, turning it this way and that, trying to understand why such things happen. In 1850—seventeen years later—he finished the poem, "In Memoriam." To me the heart of his new faith in the providence of God comes in these lines:

> O, yet we trust that somehow good
> Will be the final goal of ill,
>
> . . .
>
> That nothing walks with aimless feet;
> That not one life shall be destroy'd,
> Or cast as rubbish to the void
> When God hath made the pile complete;
>
> . . .
>
> I can but trust that good shall fall
> At last—far off—at last, to all . . .

IV

There come times—not one but many—for all when faith falters. It is as universal an experience, I suspect, as we shall find in religion. There are times when we outgrow traditional ideas—not all of them at any one time, to be sure, but some of them are certain to be challenged by every great experience that hits us or our generation. A dramatic instance of this was the remark of a disillusioned German who dismissed the traditional faith in God as a Father by saying, "That idea died in the first World War." A less dramatic but much more universal experience of challenge is to be found in the experience of someone going to college or graduate school.

College, to revert to that for a moment, is a rough experience on students, and the better the college, the rougher the experience is likely to be. I suspect my own experience is typical and not at all unusual.

I had been brought up in the tenets of a fundamentalism which held that the Bible is an infallible authority, while the earth is a cosmic stage created for the especial benefit of man. You can imagine what happened to both those ideas as soon as I got to the University!

The professor in Bible started punching the notion of Biblical infallibility all over the place. I wanted to fight back but was prevented by the slight inconvenience that he had all of the facts on his side! While I was suffering under that challenge the professor in biology was relating me to what I had previously called "the lower forms of life" in positively a revolting way! At the end of that harrowing year I knew I faced a simple choice: push on to a more adequate faith or give up religion altogether. Try as I might, I could find no third position. Nor was I alone in this kind of trouble. A classmate on graduation day with his diploma finally safely in hand said, "If I had known before I came what was going to happen to me here I would never have come." And, believe it or not, he went on into the Methodist ministry!

Imagine a chap like that trying to steady the banner of the Psalmist, or the prophets or Paul. Men like that would never understand the "Dark Night of the Soul" of the mystic, the living death of Paul or the faltering faith of the Psalmist. Nor would they be able to lift the shout, "For I am persuaded, that neither death, nor life, . . . nor things to come, . . . shall be able to separate us from the love of God."

It is always a disturbing experience to have our traditional faith challenged by new facts and experiences. Yet there is no escape from it—not even that offered by a kind of automatic dogmatism that seems to be coming into favor these days. We have been treated to a number of public instances in which people have taken refuge from doubt in the fortress of traditional authority in religion. They profess to find steadiness of soul in accepting the teachings of some one church or sect. They shout triumphantly, "This is it!"

I do not mean to be either disrespectful or intolerant when I say they remind me a little of the time our three-year-old boy came up to us on the beach with his sand bucket full of water. "Here's the ocean, Daddy," he said. That attitude is understandable in a three-year-old, but not so much so when a thirty-year-old comes up with a set of ideas and says, "Here is the truth!" You want to say to him, "That may be your ocean, but there is a lot more where that came from, and it's not in your bucket!"

Institutions as well as people face times when they must turn from traditional policies and answers in order to meet the problems of the present more adequately. Every reader of Christian history can cite a dozen times when the Church has had to do this. I have never known a time when the Church, trying as she is to minister to a broken world, needed to have a greater sense of freedom and flexibility to move in new directions than now. With National and World Council movements growing apace, we shall need to turn away from many of our denominational ways and learn how to work together in many new and deeper modes. Neither man nor any one church liveth unto itself alone any more. The leaders we need, the leaders we believe this class of graduates will provide, will know that it will take big keys, the biggest we have, to open the locked doors of a better future. The lock on the door of fear is great, but it can be opened with the key of trust. The lock on the door of greed is great, but it can be turned by the key of sharing. The lock on the door of hatred is great, but there is

a key that fits—the key of love. All these keys can be in our hands
if first they are in the hearts of Christian men and women the
world over. And despite cynics, skeptics and fainthearted ones, we
must use them now and be ready to move toward a better world
than men have ever known.

V

Let us remember then when our faith falters in this business of
living, as it will, that God's steadying hand is on our shoulder leading us on to even greater things.

Baron von Hügel discovered this about sorrow and suffering. He
communicated it to a friend in sorrow in a letter, "There is surely
for us Christians no surer test of faith on our part, no truer proof
of love on God's part, than suffering nobly born . . . and nothing
that unites and reunites at all as does such suffering."

One of the precious privileges of each generation I gladly give to
this new generation of Methodist preachers—that of continuing
your re-examination of our heritage. And I charge you with the
responsibility of being as fair to the generations to come as you
will try to be to those that have gone before. Go through our
heritage as you would your attic on moving day. (As Methodist
preachers, I can guarantee that you will become intimately acquainted with that simile!) And as you go through the heritage I
bid you keep, strengthen and augment that which is useful; modify and discard that which is not.

And keep the Church hard at the task of being the Church! Of
being the one who holds a high standard alongside personal and
social life, measuring the worth of what we are and do by the
Kingdom of God itself.

And when you falter in the task, as falter you will repeatedly,
and find yourself asking: "Will the Lord cast off forever? Is His
loving-kindness clean gone forever? Hath God forgotten to be
gracious?" remember then the necessity of moving straight ahead
toward a greater faith, knowing you will be sustained by the God
of the universe.

Some years ago when Nansen, the great Arctic explorer, was

looking for the North Pole, he found himself one day in very deep water and let down his sounding line to calculate its depth. But even when that line was all played out, it did not reach the bottom of the sea. More and more line was added until he was taking soundings with all the line he had aboard, but still he failed to reach the ocean bed. So he noted in his log book the entry, "3500 fathoms—and deeper than that!"

When our faith falters before some great task, some great locked door, some experiences of tragedy, and we ask, "Is God great enough for that?" then listen and we will hear the answer as given by those who have gone before us: "Yes, and greater than that!"

XIV

That Generations to Come May Know![1]

SCRIPTURE LESSON: Psalm 78:1–8

I

THE Church and her families come together upon occasions like this both to celebrate an important fact and to reinforce each other for inescapable encounters with mutual enemies.

The fact to be celebrated is our historic interdependence with each other. We are not strangers; we are long-standing friends and colleagues. We are intimately acquainted, knowing each other's strength and weaknesses. We need each other now as badly as ever if we are to do our duties as they need to be done. The Church cannot do without the family and the family, as we know it, would soon lose its sense of direction and strength without the Church. This fact of interdependence is important—important enough for us to come together before God, rejoicing in our unity. This we do with high faith and full heart today.

The enemies we reinforce each other to face are individualism on the one hand and collectivism on the other. Both philosophies of life are to be found in some form all through the world today, and one is as deadly an enemy of the Christian Church and the Christian home as is the other. The challenge must be faced openly; the issue must be joined consciously and fully; the battle must be fought on to victory—and Church and home need each other in the inescapable conflict.

Obviously, purposes like these will not be served if we are content to throw bouquets at each other—even bouquets dipped in

---

[1] Preached on Family Sunday.

holy water and fragrant with the incense of holy places. Something of the high seriousness which characterizes the 78th Psalm will serve us better—and it will serve us very well indeed if we will but let it. There is a refreshing honesty about it that may affect some of us like strong medicine, but we will feel better for having taken it if we do.

II

The Psalmist addresses his own people and he does so with all the power of an Amos. He knows history, but he is not enslaved by it. He respects tradition, but he does not hesitate to break with it. He knows of the sainted fathers of his people, but he describes their sins with pitiless clarity. As a matter of strict fact, he strikes me as one who is thoroughly fed up with the claptrap we usually get on historic occasions about those paragons of wisdom, of honor, of integrity, of faithfulness—our fathers before us! He has, he says, a single purpose, to "tell the coming generations the glorious deeds of the Lord" and of His Law for Israel. He hopes to do this in so compelling a fashion that they will not only hear but will also tell their children and their children's children in order that "generations to come may know" and "set their hope in God and not forget [His] works, but keep his commandments: and that they should not be like their fathers, a stubborn and rebellious generation, a generation whose heart was not steadfast, whose spirit was not faithful to God."

It is hard on fathers—I speak as one now—to be told that it would be better for all concerned if our children were not like us. Not many of us are humble enough to take that without some objection. We are more like the man, a Yale graduate, who took his son to enroll at the alma mater. He had heard the rumors about new ways and notions there, so he sought out the dean of students and told him his dream for the boy: "I want him to get exactly what I got when I was here." The dean puzzled for a moment and then asked, "You mean you want him to follow in your footsteps?" The father smilingly agreed. The dean said, "Look, now! You're a great guy and we're proud of you, but don't you think one of you is enough?" And, for one alarming moment, the dean was not sure the father was going to smile!

The ears of the fathers of Israel must have burned as the Psalmist explicitly urged his hearers not to be like them, a generation whose heart was not steadfast, whose spirit was not faithful to God. But the spirit of Hebrew prophecy rejoiced in his plea that they be loyal and grateful to God for His glorious deeds, that they love and adore Him, that they worship Him and teach their children to love and worship Him above all else.

It never occurred to the Psalmist, as it does to many of us, that his religion is a private affair, to be sucked like a spiritual lollypop at his own convenience and for his own pleasure. Rather it is a sacred trust which he may enjoy to the depths of his soul, but which he must share with others, beginning with his children. The Hebrews were a family-centered people. They might and did build great temples and synagogues, but their homes remained the beating heart of their life. For nearly twenty-six hundred years now they have learned these words of Deuteronomy much as we learn the Lord's Prayer:

Hear, O Israel: The Lord our God is one Lord and you shall love the Lord your God with all your heart, and with all your soul, and with all your might. And these words which I command you this day shall be upon your heart; and you shall teach them diligently to your children, and shall talk of them when you sit in your house, and when you walk by the way, and when you lie down, and when you rise. And you shall bind them as a sign upon your hand, and they shall be as frontlets between your eyes. And you shall write them on the doorposts of your house and on your gates.

Better than anything else this ancient commitment of the Hebrew home describes the essential difference between a religious and an irreligious home. This difference still stands. It is not needful, I am sure, to call special attention to the spiritual unity of organized religion and the home in all this! They do not ignore or neglect each other. They do not say to each other, "I have no need of thee!" Church and home need each other as together they try to teach the generations that are to come to love and worship God and to find their way in His Will. That fact we celebrate today.

And it is high time we both celebrate it and repent of our carelessness about it. For, like our fathers before us, we have become increasingly lax about the religious responsibilities of the home. We buy Bibles but we neither read them ourselves nor do we teach our children how to do so. We profess to believe in God, yet the practice of family worship in any form has long since fallen into disuse—a casualty of our carelessness or lack of concern. We belong to church, but our participation in its life is geared strictly to our own convenience, making it one of the electives or luxuries of life. We have neither the right nor the desire to present it to our children as a necessity. We want the church to have a good church school—one that will teach our children the fundamentals of our faith—but we flatly refuse to have anything to do with it ourselves. Then we wonder why our children lose interest in it when they are on their own. I confess to some weariness of soul when I hear otherwise mature people account for their lack of interest in church on the basis that "they were made to go to church too much when they were young." Not one person in a hundred can honestly document that amazing claim. Even if it were true, I doubt whether it justifies their failure to furnish their children with the encouragement of a consistent interest in religious matters.

Let us, then, by all means celebrate our awareness of the interdependence between church and home today but let us begin by confessing, "For all have sinned and come short of the glory of God."

III

I am not afraid of either individualism or collectivism if church and home once more fall to the task of telling the generations to come to love and worship God and to do so with steadfast hearts and faithful spirits. As we are successful in this, the insidious whisper of individualism that "we are gods" and the blatant claim of collectivism that the state or something else is God will receive their full answer. Let a man know that he is a child of God and he will think humbly of himself, knowing that he is no better than anyone else. Let him know that he is a child of God, and he will not be deceived by the pretensions of an omnipotent state or society. I think it no accident that Mussolini, Hitler and Lenin reached for the control of the Church with one hand and the control of the home with the other as soon as they came to power and wanted to consolidate their power. They knew they had to win both in order to survive. Home and church working together give life a meaning, a dignity, a purpose that quite transcend the effective grasp of our tyrants, and no one knows this better than the tyrants themselves.

We have an equally implacable quarrel with what has been called "rugged individualism" because of its false and dangerous separation of the individual from the intimate groups of family, church and community. Rugged individualism, as such, encourages the individual to find himself not by losing himself for the sake of others, but by isolating himself for his own sake. That way of life is as hostile to the Christian understanding of life as is communism.

I hope it will not sound either smug or complacent to say that church and home standing together are quite ready to meet all such challenges. That sounds almost too easy, doesn't it? Let me put it in a slightly different fashion, and we shall see that there is nothing easy about it. If you as a family maintain a consistent and sympathetic interest and participation in the life and work of this church, and if this church bends every effort to the task of bringing the Christian gospel to bear upon the problems of personal and social living, then we will be ready to attempt the Christian life and the Christian society. We have a right to ask the church to do her job and the church has a right to ask us to share fully in her program. To the extent that we are able to do this together, we stand in the historic tradition of those who are determined "that the generations to come may know" of the glory of God and His claim on human life.

IV

As church and home stand and work together, what, you ask, will the generations know? Many things, I am sure, but especially these.

They will know the joy of the shared life. From the day of Adam it has not been good that one should be alone. And, as well we know, a family sees to it that we are not alone! In fact, how to have privacy within a family is one of the pressing problems of family life!

On one of my first visits to Boston I was shown the home of Nathaniel Hawthorne, I think it was, in one of the suburbs of that city. It was a large house with a sharply peaked roof that was pointed out to me. And I noticed a peculiar thing on the roof of the house. Resting on one of the sides of the roof was something that looked like a large dollhouse. As I studied it I could see no steps leading up to it, so I questioned my companion. He explained that the house on the roof was Hawthorne's solution to the problem of a nagging wife. Hawthorne entered it by opening a door in the roof of the house, placing a ladder from that to a trap door in the floor of the little house. Once in the sanctuary, he would pull the ladder up after him, shut the door in the floor—and he was safe until he got hungry!

Some years ago, J. P. Marquand, one of our best novelists, was taking a reporter from *The Saturday Review* through his new home built on one of the hills of Boston. They went through two or three floors looking at bedrooms, dining rooms, kitchens, but the reporter saw no study. Finally he asked the writer about this, whereupon Mr. Marquand led him to the elevator and they dropped down to a half-basement room which was a beautifully appointed study. Mr. Marquand explained, "We put it down here so I could get away from the family and work in peace." Then he added, "But it hasn't worked out that way. They just moved down here, too!" Now that one of Mr. Marquand's sons is a novelist in his own right, I suspect that the father is glad the family moved in on his study and took it over.

The shared life sought by a family and achievable only within a family has its problems, to be sure, but it has its own rewards, too. We need it. We need to be caught up in the simple, direct, honest, human relationship of the home. A home is basically not a matter of where you live or the things you have to live among; it is a matter of personal affection, understanding and loyalty. One of my recent Sunday visits to Wellesley College coincided with Father's Day of the sophomore class. Three or four hundred fathers were attending classes, going to dinners, coming to chapel, and responding as if from habit to "Daddy this and Daddy that!" And as they got in their cars to go home I noticed that they were laden with laundry bags, sacks of everything their daughters thought they could do without for the rest of the year! And, I give you my word, I never saw a more contented group of men in my life. One of them is a Justice of the Supreme Court, another a highly placed official in government, and many equally well-known in other areas of life—but at that time they were all "fathers" and they knew no higher title because there is none.

There is more than joy in the shared life of the home. There is power—creative and re-creative power—sufficient for every demand that may be placed upon us. The power of the home is widely recognized. We have been told that the home is the last bulwark of civilization—and that is true. We have been told that the home is the most effective (whether good or bad) school we have—and that is true. Now, as a minister of the Church, I should like to add my testimony that the home is or can be the most precious sanctuary in the world. For in the home the deepest things of God are brought to fulfillment in our life.

Why should this not be true? Love is of God; love is God's hand on our shoulder and love is the foundation of our home and our family life. Love brings and holds husband and wife together, growing in grace and strength over the years. From love come children and the will to help them bring to fulfillment God's will for their lives. From love comes the strength we need to be the person we ought to be, to attempt the things we ought to attempt, to surge back from failure, to try and to keep on trying until we get the job done.

V

I do not mean that this business of building a home and keeping it under God is an easy matter. It is one of the hardest things we ever undertake. It is a staggering thing to realize that good and evil alike use the same carrier. Greater good and greater evil come through intimate personal relations than through any other channel. I tell every young couple that comes to me for marriage that we can help each other more and hurt each other worse in marriage and the home than in any other relationship we will ever have. The cruelty of parents to children and of children to parents is the keenest-edged pain known to human beings, and against that there is literally no defense.

You have heard the brutal half-truth, have you not, that "familiarity breeds contempt"? The whole truth reads, "Familiarity, without love, may breed contempt; familiarity, with love, will breed appreciation, joy and comradeship." If, and to the extent that, our intimate human relations become casual if not cruel, it is because we have lost our vision and awareness of the glory of God's love that is trying to speak to us through them. That, better than anything else, explains why it is that church and home need to stand together as these intimate human relations grow and develop through our lifetime.

One of the costs of home and family is the restraint and responsibility they bring. George Santayana has been hailed as one of the great philosophers of our generation. His last book, *My Host the World*, contains these interesting words, "To possess [things or persons] physically or legally is a burden and a snare." W. H. Auden the poet comments, "Quite so, but it is equally true that it is only through such possessions that most men can learn loyalty and responsibility. The danger is equally an opportunity, and to refuse to risk the one is to miss the other." [2]

It is, I repeat, the duty of the Church to keep these deeper truths about our shared life ever before us in the homes we have or plan to have.

[2] *Saturday Review*, April, 1953.

That is why we conclude, and rightly so, our celebration of family week with this service of consecration. Let the children and youth in our fellowship consecrate themselves to a more sensitive awareness of the richness of their homes, and of their parents' love and life. Let the parents consecrate themselves to a more sensitive awareness of the changing needs of their growing, maturing children. And let all consecrate themselves anew to the God in whom we live and move and have our being. To this end let us pray:

O God our heavenly father, in whose love we are brothers one of another and members of thy family, shed forth we pray thee thy blessed spirit of love upon all of us and especially on our homes. Make each one of us an instrument in thy hands for good. Purify our hearts, strengthen our minds and bodies; fill us with growing love for each other and for thee. Let no pride, no selfishness, no dispute, spring up among us either in our homes or in our church. Make us earnest and true, giving no cause for offense in our dealings with each other or with thee; and may thy holy peace rest upon us this day and every day cheering us in our work, strengthening us for the tasks at hand, and keeping us faithful to thee and to thy will for us now and evermore; through Jesus Christ our Lord. Amen.

XV

The Lost Secret of Great Religion

SCRIPTURE LESSON: Psalm 118:1–9, 19–24, 29

TEXT: It is better to trust in the Lord than to put confidence in man.
It is better to trust in the Lord than to put confidence in
princes.

I

In 1943 the dark and stormy night that had settled over Norway
with the occupation of the country was split by these lightning-
like words of confident reassurance:

Yes, we live in a hard time. But God is merciful even when He
chastises us. And in these last three years we have experienced His
gracious care and His powerful deeds as never before in our lives. In
the trials which have met us we have found great blessings for individuals, and they have had the greatest importance for our church. We
look back with thanks to God, and we look forward with humility—
always with trust in God.

The most significant phrase in this letter from a Norwegian
churchman to the Bishop of Copenhagen is this: "Always with
trust in God." That is the secret of the strength of religion in the
life of a person or a people.

It is an old secret—one of the oldest in religion—that men
should trust in God, and in that trust find strength sufficient for
the trials of any day. This, surely, is an ancient assurance in religious literature. It is an open secret, too. It is plain to even the

148

most casual student that the fundamental strength in religion is
confidence in God, in His mercy, in His providence, in His redemptive love.

"Trust in God?" you ask. "What is that anyway?" Is it an emotional state of peace and serenity that we reach by continuous
repetition of the words "I trust God, I trust God, I trust God"?
If so, it is a form of self-hypnosis—and no better than any of its
wretched comrades. Is it a state of peace and serenity that we
reach by stifling or ignoring or neglecting honest doubts until it
appears that everything falls into line and fits into a pattern of
ideas in terms of which we find peace of mind and peace of soul?
If so, it is intellectual dishonesty—and it is no less reprehensible
for being widely used and socially acceptable. Or is trust in God
simply a state of social conformity in the life of a religious group—
a willingness to let our doubts rest, our anxieties cease, and our life
find its peace through subordination of mind and life to the will
and way of the group? If so, it is the final capitulation of personal
responsibility and amounts to a pious acceptance of that modern
monstrosity called the "mass man."

Trust in God, as used in prophetic religion, as demonstrated by
the life and teachings of Jesus Christ, has not meant any one of
these possible perversions of it. What it *has meant*, to try to put it
in three closely related words, is this:

Trust in God means (1) Belief in God—a consciously sought,
clearly faced, factually grounded, intellectually trustworthy conviction that God is the supreme Fact and Factor in human life and
history.

Trust in God means (2) Faith in God—a belief in Him so
strong, so vital, so certain that you are willing to let it guide your
life.

Trust in God means (3) Confidence in God—a confident knowledge, born of your own experience that He can be depended upon,
that He knows and cares, that He is sufficient for all things, that
you can put the hand of your life in His outstretched hand and go
where He leads.

II

Read it any way you will, the Bible is one long document of trust in God no matter what may befall a man or a people in life. When Job cried, "Though he slay me, yet will I trust him," he was putting the secret of vital religion in an immortal phrase. Jesus knew the power of trust in God: it explains his teachings; it illuminates his life. Read again that breath-taking section on anxiety in the Sermon on the Mount: "Therefore I tell you, do not be anxious about your life, what you shall eat or what you shall drink, nor about your body, what you shall put on. Is not life more than food, and the body more than clothing? Look at the birds of the air. . . . Consider the lilies of the field. . . . If God so clothes the grass of the field, which today is alive and tomorrow is thrown into the oven, will he not much more clothe you, O men of little faith? . . . But seek first his kingdom and his righteousness, and all these things shall be yours as well." To disciples who were about to be arrested for preaching the Gospel and haled before magistrates who held the power of life and death in their hands, he counsels, "Do not be anxious how you are to speak or what you are to say; for what you are to say will be given to you in that hour; for it is not you who speak, but the Spirit of your Father speaking through you." And his own trust in God scales the heights of incredulity when he assures them that not one sparrow falls to the ground "without your Father's will . . . even the hairs on your head are all numbered. *Fear not.* . . ."

Jesus' trust in God was so patent a fact about, and so potent a force within, his life that his enemies at the Cross chose to articulate what they regarded as their triumph in terms of it. "He trusts in God," they screamed one to another. "Let God deliver him now, if he desires him; for he said, 'I am the Son of God.'" Yet even this ridicule could neither dampen his spirit nor drown out his final testament of trust: "Father, into thy hands I commit my spirit!" Jesus knew and had complete confidence in the power— the sheer power—of trust in God. He knew that it could work the impossible in human relationships. He knew, for example, that it could redeem unfaithful disciples. His final hours would have been dark indeed if he had not believed this to be true. In the early days of his ministry his disciples gathered around him eagerly; they followed him gladly; and then, in the latter days of his life when opposition was mounting and tragedy was inevitable, they faltered and finally left him—not one remaining at his side as he bore his burdens to Calvary. Yet his trust in them was not shaken. What is more, it was justified in history. He knew and they discovered that what they had learned of God through him created a fundamental confidence in themselves and their mission that redeemed them and brought them back into the stream of history as men of strength and courage. The Christian religion has been made strong not by men who never doubted, but by men whose tremendous doubts about themselves, their comrades and their mission were redeemed by an even greater faith in God.

The great figures in Christian history discovered the serenity and the strength of trust in God: Paul could emerge from many years of doubt, anguish and spiritual tragedy with this word of trust on his lips, "I know whom I have believed, and am persuaded that he is able to keep that which I have committed unto him against that day"; St. Augustine could bring his long and fretful journey through the philosophies and theologies of his day to complete peace of mind and spirit in his assurance, "Nor in all these which I review . . . find I a secure place for my soul, save in thee, into whom my scattered members may be gathered together, and nothing of me depart from thee." Luther, Wesley and a whole host of others share in the great tradition of trust in God.

Two of the most searching testimonials to the importance of this secret come from little-known figures in the fourteenth century. A mystical Dominican monk, Meister Eckhart by name, gives this as his testament of faith, "Trust and perfect love is demonstrated when a man has great hope and confidence in God. There is nothing to test the perfection of love better than trust. Wholehearted love for another person carries confidence with it. Whatever one dares to trust God for, he really finds in God and a thousand times more." Johannes Tauler, one of the great preacher-mystics of that period, has given us in an imaginative poem a conversation which he had with a stranger sent from Heaven. The stranger has been urging Tauler to have complete trust in God in all things. Tauler understandably shrinks from this and finally asks, "What if God's will consign thee hence to Hell?"

> "Then," said the stranger cheerily, "be it so.
> What Hell may be I know not; this I know—
> I cannot lose the presence of the Lord:
> One arm, Humility, takes hold upon
> His dear Humanity; the other, Love,
> Clasps His Divinity. So where I go,
> He goes; and better fire-walled Hell with Him
> Than Golden-gated Paradise without."

I have spent this much time with examples and testimonials of the meaning of trust in God in order that we may be confident of the fact that it is one of the oldest, one of the most open, one of the most important secrets of great religion in every generation.

Yet this selfsame secret of trust in God comes close to being the lost secret of our generation. This better than anything else explains the spiritual tragedy that has overtaken us and our civilization. We have trusted everyone and everything but God. We have rejected the disciplines of prophetic religion only to discover to our immeasurable sorrow that the pleasures of paganism come terribly high. We simply could not believe it when prophetic religion insisted that the only road to the good life and to the good society lay in the glorification of God's will in human life. That, we said, is too high and too hard a road. So we took counsel with ourselves and demanded to know what God had to do with it anyway! Some of us wanted to know why we could not ignore Him altogether. We said to ourselves that we could glorify life, glorify society, and forget all about God. Reasoning thus, we conjured up the pseudo-religions of humanism on the one hand, which is a glorification of life, and of totalitarianism on the other, which is a glorification of society. One would think that the tragic sacrifices which we have been forced to make in the name of these man-made and man-centered religions would label them once and for

all as the charnal houses of destruction which they are and close
them forever in the minds of thoughtful people.

III

The writer of the 118th Psalm saw something like that happening in his day. Thereupon he drew a sharp line between his faith
and that of his pagan contemporaries. To the humanist he said, "It
is better to trust in the Lord than to put confidence in man." To
the totalitarian he said, "It is better to trust in the Lord than to
put confidence in princes." There we have it: the eternal difference between man-made and man-centered religion and divinely-
inspired and divinely-centered religion! Great religion does not
begin with man and trust in man; it begins with God and trust in
God.

This kind of trust in God deserves our undivided attention in
this day of confusion. We are living at a time when high ideals are
hard to maintain; when high hopes daily grow dimmer; when men
once more are preparing to rebuild the altars of humanism and
totalitarianism and put their whole confidence in man-made de-
vices—treaties and institutions—thinking somehow or other by
man-made wisdom and his might to guarantee to our generation
something that no other generation has ever been able in its own
wisdom and might to win for itself. Before we start once more on
what has always been a one-way trip to disaster, it surely is the part
of wisdom to investigate more carefully the survival and redemptive value of placing our whole trust in God. Trust in God is not
divorced from ordinary living. You do not have to lift your eyes to
the cloudlands of dreams in order to discover it. Like all great religious declarations, it is rooted and grounded in daily living. You
simply cannot live without trust.

Try being skeptical about everyone and everything and see how
long it is possible for you to live! I find it simply impossible to
enumerate the number of persons I have trusted, consciously or
not, in making any trip. My safety, well-being, peace of mind and
ability to move from place to place—all these have been made
possible by tens of thousands of other people who were no more

aware of me personally than I was of them. I go into the food market and ask for a cut of meat weighing four or five pounds. I trust the butcher, the man who checks the scales, the Pure Food and Drug Laws that hover over the entire transaction. Trust, acknowledged or unacknowledged, in people, known or unknown, is the very atmosphere in which we move. Try being skeptical about it all and you simply declare yourselves out of the entire human enterprise. The great problem in daily living is not that of creating trust among people from the ground up; rather it is that of increasing the essential element of trust already in existence until it is sufficient for the truly critical problems that we face in our total relationships with other people.

"Trust everyone and anyone?" you ask. "There are untrustworthy people in this world, you know." The secret of trust in other people is most important at the very points where it is most difficult—the points where it has been betrayed. There is no magic known to man that can keep trust from being betrayed upon occasion. When this happens, whether between husband and wife, parent and child, colleague or friend, the normal human reaction is to pronounce a thundering judgment upon the sinner, break the relationship off, and try to forget the whole wretched business. This, I say, is the normal human reaction, but it is far from being a profoundly Christian one. The parable of the prodigal son points to a quite different kind of reaction, does it not? And so does the prayer, "Father, forgive them; for they know not what they do." Dr. Reinhold Niebuhr wisely observes, "The only whole relationship is a healed one." We must learn how to master the tragedy of trust betrayed—and pray to God that those who love us can master it too. For we too will sin against them in some way or other sooner or later. While great religion seeks to lift life to a level of integrity and loyalty that will keep such betrayals at minimum, it knows they will happen and is prepared to redeem them.

What I am saying amounts to this: the only known way of redeeming a trust betrayed in human relationships begins with an affirmation of a vital trust in God. Among the many things that trust in God may mean, certain ones stand out: it means a forgiv-

community good will and trust, and He is our ally. One thing is sure: God is not neutral. Where these breaches exist in human relationships, God is not just on one side pushing at somebody; He is on both sides trying to bring people together. His love and purpose for all men are our deepest guarantees that our efforts for world community will finally be successful. Just now it is infinitely more important for us to create a new trust in one another through encouraging a greater trust in God than it is for us to build atomic bombs or maintain a huge standing army.

We have been warned by those who know that trust in one another is of the very essence of our salvation as a civilization. Lord Boyd Orr, winner of the Nobel Peace Prize in 1949, writes,

We are in the middle of the greatest and most rapid transition phase in the evolution of human society. We can go forward but we cannot go back. To fight to maintain the Status Quo is to invite defeat. To us a biological metaphor, the chrysalis may evolve into a butterfly, or it may die, but it cannot reverse the process of change and become a caterpillar again.[1]

Trust—the kind we need—will give us both the power to let go of our fears and move ahead with our faith.

[1] Nation, May 20, 1950.

XVI

Wanted: An Unpurchasable Man!

SCRIPTURE LESSON: Psalm 121:1–8 and Psalm 127:1

I

DURING October, 1947, the New York *Herald Tribune* held its annual forum on world affairs in New York City. Convened in the Waldorf-Astoria Hotel were some of the outstanding men of science, philosophy, government, the press, labor, education and religion. As you might expect, they addressed themselves to no mean theme! Their subject was "Modern Man: Slave or Sovereign." The full newspaper account of the meeting made it abundantly clear that this was no complacent gathering of smug people who faced present and future with unruffled confidence that everything would turn out all right for us and our world. Everyone there was standing in the shadow of two clouds—and he knew it! There was the rising storm of conflict in the United Nations between Russia and the United States: a conflict for which both were clearly responsible and which threatened the very future of the United Nations itself. The second was a mushroom cloud that presaged the early and complete end of modern man and all his works if ever he becomes involved in another major war. Thinking and planning in such an atmosphere is guaranteed to make a man as sober as the fabled owl. And the people at this forum were sober! I have read the records of many a solemn conference on great issues, but, for sheer seriousness, none topped this one in New York City.

All wanted modern civilization to survive. All believed that it could, though not in its present form, which has been fashioned too much on the anvils of war and too little in the councils of peace. All believed that modern man had the resources to redesign and rebuild his tottering world. But all doubted whether he was willing to do it. All agreed in this—the most important conclusion of the conference—that "the basic spiritual values that are mankind's heritage from the past alone can assure the survival of human freedom in today's menaced world." This is not a new conclusion—nor was it advanced by the conference as such. But it would be utterly tragic if we permitted its triteness to disguise its urgency. Better than anything else it speaks to the heart of our time.

What this group of intelligent, thoughtful leaders from every walk of life said is what prophetic religion has been saying to beleaguered men and bedeviled generations for over three thousand years. To put it in prophetic parlance, "There is a way out—but it is God's way, not yours. Unless you make it yours, you are hopelessly lost. If you do make it yours, you will need every ounce of spiritual strength you can find in order to follow it, but if you follow it faithfully, it will lead to victory."

II

Two of the best-known statements of this prophetic faith occur, one in the Old and the other in the New Testament of our Bible. We have heard them both many times. The Psalmist exclaims, "Except the Lord build the house, they labour in vain that build it; except the Lord keep the city, the watchman waketh but in vain." The writer of I John puts it even more succinctly: "Whatsoever is born of God overcometh the world."

This faith in God as the most important Fact and Factor in life lies at the heart of all of the spiritual values which we are being told—and rightly—that we must recover or perish. We need and want to believe in the dignity of man, yet we cannot except we believe in the divinity of man, that is, his sonship to the living God. We want to believe in one world, yet we cannot except we are able to believe in the brotherhood of man and the Kingdom of God. Struggling as we are to overcome the accumulated evils of history before they overcome us, trying as we are to build a new world—a better world than men have ever known before—we must be prepared to begin at the beginning—which, in our religious tradition, means, "In the beginning, God. . . ." There is no other starting point for the victory we seek as Christian men and women. Yet to begin here and carry through logically to its conclusion will be far from easy.

For one thing, the pagans and the worldlings of every generation, including our own, have challenged religion's insistence upon the fundamental nature and necessity of faith in God. When the Psalmist, watching Jerusalem in the throes of rebuilding houses and cities after the devastations of war, cried out, "Except the Lord build the house, they labour in vain that build it; except the Lord keep the city, the watchman waketh but in vain," the worldling and the pagan of that day had a ready answer. He could say in substance, "The security of this city lies in two things: the strength of our walls and the vigilance of our watchmen. Both these are dependent upon us, not upon God. Faith in God is all right for those who want it, but it will not build and man the walls of this city, and we are dependent upon these things for security."

But the Psalmist's meaning is clear: "It doesn't make any difference about our walls and our watchmen if our purpose is evil and our common life is honeycombed with injustice and unrighteousness. The true strength of the city lies in having the right kind of persons in the right kind of common life. Without these our walls will either be breached in battle for lack of defenders or they will crumble away in disrepair because no one is concerned about them."

The writer of I John faced much the same situation when at a much later date he cried, "Whatsoever is born of God overcometh the world!" He lived in one of the great days of the Roman Empire. Rome was so big, so powerful, that to early Christians she was the symbol of "the world." The worldling and the pagan of that day must have thought the writer of our little missive wholly out of his mind! He could cry to him, "The things that really endure are power and wealth. They constitute stability and order. They are the symbols of authority and law. Whether they are right or wrong, good or evil, are academic questions, at best. What really counts is the simple fact that they alone really matter in this world. Your queer religion may label them evil but they have put your Christ to the cross, your churches to the torch, and your leaders to the torture chambers. They have driven you out of the public places into exile or into hiding. You have no power—not even that of your God—that can equal their authority in life."

The writer of I John knew all this—and disbelieved it to the bottom of his heart: "No—the Caesars and their power will pass away if they do not learn to serve the living God. If they do not find their way in the will of God they will perish. No man, no nation, however great, can oppose God and live. What God wills is the most powerful, the only irresistible purpose in the world. If we live in line with it, something of its power comes into our life. And with that power we can overcome the world—even Rome! The victory we seek is to be found in God's will for the world and in nothing less or other than that!"

The pagans of our day—if they think at all—cannot help being sobered by the fact that in these historic instances their spiritual forerunners were wrong—dead wrong! Injustice and unrighteousness had destroyed Jerusalem as a community before the battering rams of Pompey ever approached the city! A many-factioned thrust for power had made Rome the scene of continuous civil war long before the Goths swept in and took over.

Over and over again—and never more dramatically than in our own day—this great insight of prophetic religion has been upheld in history: When a man or a people ground their life in God, they will be accounted victors, if not in their own day, then by subsequent generations. I repeat: Struggling as we are to overcome the accumulated evils of history before they overcome us, trying as we are to build a new and fairer world than men have ever known before, we must be prepared to begin at the true beginning of all creative and stable efforts and accomplishments—"In the beginning, God. . . ."

III

Well and good, you say, as an ideal, as a vision, as the over-all picture toward which we may glance once in a while when our spirits are low—but where do I as a person come into it today? What does it mean to me, here and now?

These are good questions, and they deserve as honest an answer as we can find. Better than any other contemporary writer, William Ernest Hocking of Harvard has tried to put down in black and white what religion is trying to do in and through human beings. He writes,

Only religion can create the unpurchasable man. And it is only the man unpurchasable by society that can create a sound society. And the society of unpurchasable men, with a moral anchor outside their own national life, is the only society that can beget world unity.[1]

There—in a single, lucid statement—is what religion is about and why it centers its life and faith in God. The charge that religion is preoccupied with another world is true insofar as religion is concerned with this world as it ought to be. So far from being content with lovely dreams of what this world ought to be, religion, beginning with people neither better nor wiser than we are, is trying to create the kind of people who can build that kind of world. In a sentence, religion is trying to create unpurchasable men.

I know—many of our contemporaries take a dim view of man and scoff at the suggestion that there is any such creature as an unpurchasable man. Every man has his price, they say; find it and pay it, and you have him! They are like the captain who was charged with maintaining a blockade of one of the Southern ports during the Civil War. Some blockade runners had approached him with a huge bribe if he would turn his back while they got their ships past his guard. He said "No" to their first overture. They increased the bribe—he said "No" again. They increased the bribe a third time and he jumped to his feet, saying, "Get out! You are getting too near my price!"

[1] Saturday Review of Literature, Feb. 2, 1946.

All who think there is no such thing as an unpurchasable man reason like the political leader in one of our large Northern cities who sent his henchman to find out what a very relentless critic wanted. His instructions to the henchman were, "Find out what he wants. Give it to him if you can. Anything to get him quiet." The henchman returned with a troubled countenance, "He says he wants good government." "He must be crazy!" snorted the political leader.

When people say there is no such thing as an unpurchasable man, they ought to know who some of their more noted colleagues are. I pass over Huey Long, Adolph Hitler, and every other so-called master politician, and call their attention to Satan in the Book of Job! You will recall that Satan had questioned God's confidence in Job and had said, "Let me work on him—his possessions, his relatives, his person—and sooner or later I will find out how to get him to serve me rather than you. He has his price, you know!"

IV

You ask, "What do you mean by an unpurchasable man? Put it in concrete terms! Get down to cases!" And I would like to do just that.

An unpurchasable man is one who consciously and humbly seeks to center his life in God. He believes in God. He believes in the reality of God's will for him and for all men. He believes that he is a trustee of God for the life he has and the use he makes of it. The unpurchasable man is one who knows that the most important question that can be put to a proposition or policy is whether it is in line with the will of God. Like the Psalmist, he knows that safety and security lie in the will of God and nowhere else.

The unpurchasable man can be distinguished by certain general tokens. In the first place, he cannot be bribed or flattered or frightened into a course of action which he believes to be wrong. He will stand for what he believes to be right to the very end. If you argue that this is the description of a fanatic, I shall not object. As a matter of cold fact, the difference between the prophet and the fanatic at the moment and the point of their emergence into history is practically indistinguishable. That, better than anything else, is why it behooves a troubled, chaotic society like our own to deal gently with all men and movements who seek to change the status quo. The patient scrutiny of history usually reveals the wide differences which actually separate the prophet from the fanatic. But at the moment when we must make a decision we do not have the resources of future history at our disposal. Unless we proceed carefully we shall find that, like our fathers before us, we are putting to death those who will be hailed as prophets by oncoming generations.

The second token of the unpurchasable man is this: His word will be his bond. His yea will be yea and his nay will be nay. I have always had the greatest sympathy with the line of reasoning of the early Quakers who refused to take the oath to tell the truth, the whole truth, and nothing but the truth, when they testified in civil court. They said that to take this oath would be to imply that they were not trying to tell the truth, the whole truth, and nothing but the truth any other time—and they objected to this implication. The unpurchasable man will be greatly concerned about what has been called "this little matter of integrity." He will try to make only those statements that he can stand squarely behind. He will try to be found only in those positions which he can defend, if need be, with his life.

Just at the moment, I am quite certain that one of the gravest moral dangers confronting democracy lies in our having forgotten this necessity of good citizenship. We must recapture our faith in the spoken word, in the clearly articulated policy of candidates seeking office, if democracy is to survive. While a little cynicism about political behavior is a good thing, there is altogether too much of it abroad these days to bode well for the future of democracy in this country. The sharp distinction we draw between what a candidate promises and what we expect the successful candidate to fulfill once he gets in office, points up what I mean. Until we hold our successful candidates to a more strict accounting than we have been willing or able to do in the recent past, we cannot expect any resurgence of fundamental health in democracy.

A third token of the unpurchasable man is this: He will assume personal responsibility for facing the great issues of his day. This is not and never has been easy. Many, if not most people, share the attitude of a group of high school students that invited me to talk to one of their assemblies. One of them put the request this way: "We want you to talk about some of the little problems of the day—not the big ones that we can't do anything about!"

But all of the vital problems of our time have a way of running out to the very ends of the earth! We can find provincial and parochial answers all right, answers born of our ignorance, self-righteousness and prejudice. There is a superabundance of such answers abroad today—the only trouble is they do not fit the problems we face. They are like a mechanic whom we called to help us with a motor on our boat. He unrolled as fine a kit of new tools as I have ever seen. The only trouble was that none of his wrenches would fit the crucial nut. And, in like manner, a provincial answer will not fit a universal problem. We who call ourselves Christian and seek to stand in the household of a universal faith must assume (and we have every right to expect this and every other Christian congregation to assume) a full measure of personal responsibility for facing the great issues of our time.

V

One of the greatest stories coming out of the public life of America centers in the declining years of John Quincy Adams—the only President of the United States to seek public office after his departure from the White House. He fought steadily for a widening of Democratic powers in Congress and frequently stood alone. Certainly he was the target of some of the bitterest shafts ever aimed at any man in the Congress. Upon one occasion a session of the Congress was assembling in Washington and trying to get organized. There were two delegations from New Jersey seeking recognition as the lawful representatives of that state. The division in voting in Congress on critical issues promised to be close, and one faction favored one delegation and the other faction favored another. As a result of some political maneuvering the clerk who was calling the roll of the House was instructed to declare that the House was not in session until one of the factions from New Jersey had been seated, and so long as two were presenting themselves there looked to be no answer to the dilemma. For four days the clerk monotonously called the roll of the House and then would declare that the House was not in session because the delegates from New Jersey were not present. Finally, the aged Adams arose and demanded that the question be put as to who were the representatives from New Jersey. His colleagues round about him, none of whom was willing to take the political risk involved in putting the question, turned to him and demanded to know, "Who will put the question?" Adams replied, "I intend to put that question myself." And he did! And the Congress was duly organized in short order because he was willing to assume the responsibility.

You and I want labor and management to find a new basis for co-operation in building a stable social order. Very well: So does everyone else. But are we willing to put the question ourselves? You and I are anxious for the racial groups of the world to learn to live in peace and harmony with one another. Very well. But are we willing to put the necessary questions ourselves? We want the great nations of the earth to accept such limitations of their sovereignty as will be necessary for the United Nations to grow in strength and usefulness. And we do well! But are we prepared to put the necessary questions to our own nation ourselves? Living as we do in as powerful and as self-righteous and as implacably sovereign a nation as exists on the face of the earth—are we willing to put the question which will cause our people to think seriously and finally modify our traditional position on this matter? We want the nations of this earth to embrace disarmament under the guidance of the United Nations. We want to stop plowing eighty-five cents out of every dollar into armaments, past, present and future. So does every normal person who has the slightest appreciation of what another war might mean. But are we prepared to put the question to the nations, beginning with our own, ourselves? Or are we going to be led like sheep to another slaughter simply because an increasing number of us will not assume the personal responsibility of initiating new and profound reversals of traditional actions and reactions on this matter?

Unpurchasable men may be few and far between, but they are not unknown. I have known some who are the solid core of strength in our religious tradition—and so have you. I think of Moses before Pharaoh, Jesus before Pilate, Luther before the holy Roman Emperor, John Bunyan before the courts of England, Pastor Niemoeller before Hitler. Men like these have been the dividing points in history from the very beginning of our tradition —and they always will be. For they are the voice of God to the common life of mankind. This is their glory and our tragedy: These unpurchasable men were persons like us made different by the absoluteness of their loyalty to the will of God. They were not content merely to hurl defiance at the status quo—though they did that; they sought to insert themselves as instruments of divine redemption in the life of their day. They were willing to lose themselves, in good New Testament fashion, in order to find themselves. And so must we be!

We seek a new society. Not one born of man but born of God. One in which every person will be treated as a child of God, as the bearer of intrinsic worth. We seek a creative, dynamic society where changes are expected, encouraged and cultivated to the end that men will dwell together in security and community.

We seek the kind of church that will spearhead the thrust toward a new society. Not a congregation of timid craven people who are afraid of their own shadow, much less their own faith; who, mouthing great convictions Sunday after Sunday, are quite loath to implement those convictions in terms of social institutions and political behavior. We have altogether too many churches like this just now! What we want and what we need if we are ever to build a new society is the kind of church which will take seriously the convictions which in the first century did overturn the world, and if taken seriously again, will certainly remake the world once more. No one of us alone and no portion of the Christian Church by itself can do this mighty task in our generation. But six hundred million of us standing together, thinking together, praying together, working together for the glory of God and for the redemption of the world cannot long be denied. We must be willing to bring the will of God, as we understand it, into a creative relationship with the great issues of our day, as we see them—believing that in and through that effort the will of God will find new entrance into human life. This is our clear and Christian responsibility. And, as surely as God lives, the efforts to do this will for us, as for the Psalmist and for the writer of I John, be blessed with the kind of victory which alone we seek.

XVII

Backward, Turn Backward!

SCRIPTURE LESSON: Psalm 137:1–6

I

ONE of the most frequent criticisms of the Church is to the effect that she spends so much time studying yesterday that she has little time left for today and tomorrow. Professional educators, studying the curriculum of most churches, have been pointing this out for some time. And we meet the substance of the same criticism from among our own people. Try and set up an adult education program in the church, and you are sure to be advised that people will be interested in it if it deals with present-day problems, but not if it deals with the Bible or church history or theological ideas. "It's got to be alive," you are told—the inference being that the Past is dead.

Sometimes and on some issues I confess I wish the Past were dead, but wishing it lacks a lot of making it so. Actually, on many issues the Past is the liveliest, most meaningful part of the Present —and not always for good. The Past is inescapable and that is why we need to learn how to live with it, how to use rather than misuse it. It is either that or we will be done to death by it.

Therefore, one of the most important distinctions to know and always to keep in mind is this: there is a right and a wrong way to travel the lanes of memory, to hark back to "the dear dead days beyond recall," to use one's heritage and tradition. It is especially urgent that we who live in so troubled a period in human history recognize both this distinction and its importance. For one of the sure signs of a time of trouble for individual or society alike is this reference to the Past, this falling back on our tradition, this recourse to the reserves of our heritage.

As conducted—or misconducted—by many of us, this operation is little more than a pell-mell retreat from the present into the past. Properly conducted—and it can be properly conducted—it is simply and essentially a marshaling of the wisdom, insight and strength won by our fathers before us and now available to us if we learn how to use it. Nor is this distinction a mere matter of words. It results in two radically different ways of life. Two poems —one modern, the other very old—illustrate this difference.

In 1860 Elizabeth Akers Allen published the poem, "Rock Me to Sleep." It must have had a wide vogue then because it found its way into the schoolbooks of a later period. I know—because I found myself reciting it at some public function of the rural school which I attended. At the tender age of six—and enjoying life to the full, I must say—I found myself declaiming:

> Backward, turn backward, O Time, in your flight,
> Make me a child again just for tonight.
> Backward, flow backward, O tide of the years!
> I am so weary of toil and of tears.
> Toil without recompense, tears all in vain—
> Take them and give me my childhood again!

My immediate quarrel with these lines does not grow out of their sentimentalism which is strictly of the golden bantam variety. It is the simple fact that the poet is engaging in and recommending a flagrant misuse of tradition and heritage. It is one thing, and understandably human, to travel the lanes of memory back to the hills and dales of a happy childhood. It is a quite different matter, morally and spiritually speaking, to want to live there and thus to evade the toil and tears of present duties.

The other and much older poem to which I referred is the 137th Psalm. It was written during the Exile and its usefulness for us today depends upon our understanding what the Exile was and meant to the Hebrews.

The Exile began with the destruction of Jerusalem in 586 B.C. and the deportation of every actual and potential leader of the Hebrews to Babylon. It was easily the most shocking experience endured by the Hebrews. It ran counter to everything they believed about themselves, their homeland and the future. For centuries they had been taught and had taught their children that Palestine was the Promised Land given to them by God; that Jerusalem was the Holy City, protected finally by God; that the Temple was the dwelling place of the Most High and therefore beyond the reach of the profane hands of human destroyers. During the glorious years of David and Solomon such beliefs were taken for granted. Then came the time of troubles for Israel. Civil war weakened the land. The two tiny kingdoms that emerged from that war soon were minor pawns in the chess game being played by Assyria and Babylon to the Northeast and Egypt to the South. The Northern Kingdom was demolished by Assyria in 721 B.C. and its leaders were destroyed or scattered so widely they were never heard from again, except in feverish legends about the ten lost tribes of Israel. In 586 B.C. the armies of Babylon did the same thing to the Southern Kingdom, with the notable exception that we know a great deal from and about the Hebrews who were carried into Exile in Babylon. The classic lament of the 137th Psalm came from this group:

By the rivers of Babylon, there we sat down, yea, we wept, when we remembered Zion.
We hanged our harps upon the willows in the midst thereof.
For there they that carried us away captive required of us a song; and they that wasted us required of us mirth, saying, Sing us one of the songs of Zion.
How shall we sing the Lord's song in a strange land?
If I forget thee, O Jerusalem, let my right hand forget her cunning.
If I do not remember thee, let my tongue cleave to the roof of my mouth; if I prefer not Jerusalem above my chief joy.

But it would be a mistake to assume that all Exiles shared this lament. As a matter of fact, three distinct points of view and, in time, three quite different groups developed among them.

The first were those who longed for Jerusalem, who refused to accept the fact that they would be separated from Jerusalem for long, who confidently looked forward to their early return. Their loyalty to their homeland and ancestral ways was so strong that they had carried sacks of sacred soil from the Temple all those weary miles from Jerusalem to Babylon, on which to kneel and pray, facing in the direction of the Holy City.

The second group probably called themselves hardheaded realists or practical men of affairs. But whatever they called themselves, what they did, speaks for itself. They accepted the fact that they were in Babylon; they could find no reason to believe in deliverance from Babylon; they knew that Israel's power had been broken, and like most people living at that time, thought that the god of the Babylonians had overpowered the God of Israel. So—they forgot Jerusalem and the God of their Fathers. They dismissed the golden dreams of their fathers as delusions and settled down to be good Babylonians and to learn new ways of worship.

The third group mediated between these two. They, too, had to accept the bitter facts of defeat and deportation, but they could not give up either the worship of the God of their Fathers or the hope of and plan for an eventual return to Jerusalem. Even as they planned to make themselves at home in Babylon, they firmly believed that God, in His own good time, would call them forth again, and they confidently planned to be ready to hear and heed the call when it came.

Thus the Exile was truly a period of both a searching of heart and a searching of history for the exiled Hebrews. Some were content to recall the Past in order to bewail it and thus blot out the Present. Others sought to forget the Past completely and to live in the Present. A few wanted to find their strength for living in the Present in their heritage of hope which overarched Past, Present and Future alike. Understandably, then, they turned their undivided attention to the history of ancient Israel.

One of Germany's great Old Testament scholars has provided this summary of the efforts of this last group:

They studied past events from the point of view that if you do not turn away from the deeds of your fathers, then you and your children will share your ancestor's fate; if you would gain a better lot for yourselves and for your children, then you must see to it that you are not minded like your fathers. . . . This entire literature furnishes evidence of a proceeding almost unknown in history. A nation, or at least the dominant factor of it, consciously turned away from its past usage because it realized that it had followed wrong ideals. It plowed a new field, consciously brought forth a new spirit, the spirit of self-examination and understanding of themselves. It is the greatest example known to history of the renaissance of a nation from within. . . . This kept the nation alive in Babylon and inspired it with the strength to rise from humiliation and collapse. . . .[1]

When Ezra and Nehemiah came along many years later in search of men to rebuild Jerusalem these men were ready!

There you have the right way to use a heritage! That is what history and experience are for; that is why they are essential and invaluable—especially to a people in trouble. And it is just possible that could we learn to use our heritage in some such fashion, we should find the strength and leading we need today.

II

We are not responsible for our ancestors, but we are responsible for the use we make of them. We cannot avoid inheriting some tradition or other, but we can avoid the thoughtless and careless misuse of it. We are not responsible for what we inherit, but we are responsible, at least in part, for what we share with our comrades and transmit to our children. This, as we have been noting, is one of the most perplexing problems we face.

Churches must face it continually. We inherit—we cannot help inheriting—a long, rich, religious tradition; one that encompasses at least thirty-five hundred years of human experience. Unless we are wholly bereft of good judgment, we must evaluate and use that tradition in some fashion or other. The very complexity of the undertaking makes it inevitable that we shall be spending a great

[1] Gerhard Kittel, *Great Men and Movements in Israel*, Macmillan, 1929, pp. 372–73.

deal of time on it. Yet this need not and should not mean that we are more concerned with the Past than with the Present. All it need mean is that we believe we can learn much from the experiences of our religious ancestors. If we are slavish about it and content ourselves with mouthing their convictions and aping their customs as though they were the last word in the matter, we shall have misused our inheritance in an incredible fashion. Our fathers before us felt that they could understand, profit by, and improve upon their fathers—and so must we if we would be worthy heirs.

Every church had its beginnings in some such experience. The early Christians, for example, were not passive recipients of the religious heritage of Judaism. Nor were they in a state of complete rebellion against it. The New Testament makes it clear that they believed that they were more loyal to the faith of their fathers in accepting Jesus as the Messiah than were the Jews who rejected him. They had no notion that they were cutting themselves off from the hallowed traditions of Israel; not even when they were cast out of Judaism, bag and baggage, over the first two hundred years. They referred to themselves as "the new Israel." They kept the Scriptures of Judaism, the order of synagogue worship, and adhered strictly to the high moral code of Judaism. These they cherished even as the tides of history swept the Christian movement farther and farther away from Judaism.

Paul's letters are vivid chronicles of this long struggle both to inherit the traditions of Judaism yet not lose the new freedom and faith found in Jesus Christ. His letter to the Galatians has been well named "the Emancipation Proclamation" of the early Christian movement. Even though it rejects in ringing fashion slavish acceptance of Judaism, it never so much as breathes a suggestion that the main lines and the great precepts of the Hebrew heritage are to be discarded; some of the major ones are placed in a wholly new setting, but the lines of communication with the traditions running back to Moses are all up and open.

While no one can say for sure what would have been the result had Paul and his comrades let go of their Hebrew heritage, this, I am convinced, is a reasonable prophecy: they would have lost that absolute sense of direction which enabled them and their followers to thread their way through the mazes of one culture after another over the next two thousand years. They would have been letting go of that sense of continuity which has come to be one of the strongest things about the Christian faith through the ages.

Stand on any frontier today with our missionaries, and you sense the irreplaceable power of that conviction. In 1951 I talked with a young Brazilian preacher who had as his parish an area almost as large as the State of Illinois, and it was on the very rim of the jungle. Like the circuit riders in early America he does most of his traveling on horseback, dreaming of the day when he can afford a jeep. But he brushed off my sympathies with a laugh, "Paul had a much bigger parish, you know."

I will not say that that young man would not go about his duties if he could not sense his spiritual companionship with Paul and Wesley and his forefathers in the faith in Brazil, but I do say that he goes about them with greater confidence, power and sheer joy of soul because he is standing in a great missionary tradition. When he is off on his long, lonely and frequently dangerous treks, he is not alone—and he knows it. His Master is at his side and he is surrounded by a company of witnesses whose presence sustains him at all times. Tell him that the Christian tradition is dead, that it is an indication of moral and spiritual weakness to rely on your religious heritage, and his life will give you your answer. He and thousands like him are writing a new chapter in Christian history —one bearing the title "The Acts of the Apostles in Latin America." Do you wonder that he and his comrades are building what is rightly called "the fastest growing church in the world today"? This, of course, is the open secret of the continuing power of the Christian faith in human affairs. Our heritage is not a collection of dead people, dead ideas and dead institutions. It is vibrant with people, ideas and institutions that are alive, pulsing with meaning and purpose.

I do not mean that our heritage is entirely good and ought to be revered in toto. That distinctly is not the case. There are lights and shadows all through it; it is a crisscross of fact and fancy, of sound judgment and sheer superstition, of good and evil. The careful judicious study which is necessary to an understanding of the Bible is equally necessary in every other area of our heritage. That is why, like the Exiles in Babylon, we must weigh the value of what we receive in our inheritance. That is why, like the early Christians, we must hold to the main lines of our heritage yet feel free to interpret it to, and in terms of, our life and times.

III

Of this we may be sure: there are no reverse gears in life and history. As Thomas Wolfe saw and said, "You can't go home again." Your home—your entire home, spiritual as well as physical —is where you are; it is a part of all that you are and you are a part of it. When you acknowledge, accept and evaluate your religious heritage, you are not journeying into the Past; you are probing deeply for the truth of the Present. One of the probes you use is the experience of your forbears; another is your own experience; and the poverty or richness of your life is the only known measure of the wisdom and devotion with which you have done your job.

When we in our homes and church teach our children to respect, understand and study the Bible and to come to grips with the Christian view of life, we are not inviting them to run away from present responsibilities, moaning, "Backward, turn backward, O Time, in your flight." Rather we are seeking to give them an intelligent mastery of our and their spiritual heritage. We do this not in order to divert their minds from the pressing issues before us today, but in order to prepare them for these issues by sharing with them that absolute sense of direction and value which has been the token of Christian living through the ages—and which we sorely need today.

Home and church will need to work together at this great task with a new consciousness of comradeship in a common duty. We in the Church cannot perform—and I do not see how any thoughtful person could expect us to perform—the impossible task of understanding and transmitting so great an inheritance without the serious and sustained co-operation of the homes of our members and friends. The home has a right to call on the Church for leadership and continual help and, by the same token, we have a right and a duty to call on the home for co-operation all along the line. When our children seem to lose their grip on the Christian heritage—as so many are doing these days—home and Church alike must face the indictment of inadequacy. I find myself not so much provoked as perplexed when parents who have at best only a casual concern in the actual life of the Church complain because their children seem to drift away from the Church. Even so, the Church must assume her share of blame in such matters. I would remind you who now are as well as you who will become parents that the home and family are the greatest institutions on earth for the transmission of a vital religious heritage. You can do there things we cannot even attempt in the more formal institution and life of the Church, and, if you are careless or negligent or out of sympathy with the Church, you can undo there everything or nearly everything we try to do in the Church. I do not mean thereby to shirk or minimize the responsibility of the Church in these matters, but I do want to underscore the urgency and importance of the role of the home in them.

Thanks be to God, we have not yet been separated from our homeland, as were the Exiles when they sat down by the rivers of Babylon and wept, but many of us have suffered a far more grievous loss than they: we have become separated from our religious heritage; we have lost our sense of the worth of our own life and effort. That, in short, is what it means to lose our religious heritage.

The loss is grievous but not irrevocable—the heritage can be reclaimed if we are willing to make the effort. If we are willing to make it the subject of our conversation and the substance of our life, then, as God lives, the future is secure, and in that faith we can take the issues and the problems of the day as they come— and we can take them in our stride. That is what it means to be a responsible participant in a vital religious tradition.

XVIII

We Break New Seas!

Scripture Lesson: Psalm 139:1–18

Text: . . . and lead me in the way everlasting.

I

HAVE you ever asked why it is we reach so eagerly and respond so readily to stories of adventure and exploration, and why we all but idolize our adventurers and explorers? Why is it they are able to throw a spell over us with their tales of faraway places and peoples?

Boredom and envy might be given as two explanations of our excitement, but I'm convinced that the answer lies much deeper than either of these. Successful adventurers and explorers reassure us, and we need their reassurance because we are explorers all—whether we admit it or not, whether we like it or not. We are either pushing ahead or being shoved into the unknown future, and we both honor them and encourage ourselves when we pay our tribute of praise to men like Columbus.

Some poet has pictured Columbus facing westward on the bow of his ship encouraging his men with these brave words:

> We break new seas today.

They were doing that, of course. But a contemporary historian, Professor Samuel Eliot Morison, gives us an even deeper insight into what they were doing. In the preface to his biography of Columbus, he claims that Columbus not only discovered a new world but by that discovery he rescued Europe from one of her darkest moods of pessimism.

At the end of the year 1492 most men in Western Europe felt exceedingly gloomy about the future. Christian civilization appeared to be shrinking in area and dividing into hostile units as its sphere contracted. . . . Institutions were decaying and many intelligent men, for want of something better to do, were endeavoring to escape the present through studying the pagan past. . . .

The Nuremberg Chronicle, dated July 12, 1492, figured that the world would come to an end in 1493. Yet even as these gloomy predictions were being printed,

A Spanish caravel named Nina scudded before a winter's gale into Lisbon, with the news of a discovery that was to give old Europe another chance. In a few years we find the mental picture completely changed . . . New ideas flare up . . . faith in God revives and the human spirit is renewed. The change is complete and astounding. A new envisagement of the world has begun. And men are no longer sighing after the imaginary golden age that lay in the distant past, but speculating as to the golden age that might possibly lie in the oncoming future.[1]

Not many of us are inclined to minimize the importance of the adventure and discovery of Columbus either to his day or to our own. Nor do I want to appear to be doing that in calling attention to a greater explorer and to an infinitely greater exploration than his. The name of that explorer, I am sorry to report, has been lost, but the record of his exploration, thank God, is well known and widely available, being, in fact, the 139th Psalm.

Here, indeed, is a man with a mission. To put it briefly, he was determined to find a place in the universe where he could do exactly as he pleased, where he could be his own boss, where he could live on a perfectly horizontal plane all the livelong day. He was trying to find some place where he could get away from God. Like many another man before and since, he was quite sure he could get along without God.

If we are to place any credence in the record—and, I confess, it

---

[1] Samuel Eliot Morison, *Admiral of the Ocean Sea.* Little, Brown, 1942, p. 3.

seems to be a very sincere report—he made every effort to succeed. But, in so doing, *he made a tremendous discovery not only about God's place in the universe, but also about his place in God's universe.* Wherever he went in order to escape God, he found that not only was God there but also that God had been with him every step of the journey. And then it dawned on him as definitely as the new world rose up in the west to greet Columbus that God knew him better than he knew himself, that God had created him in his mother's womb; that God had surrounded him with His purpose and even now was seeking to guide him. He discovered God to be both an infinite fact about the objective universe and the intimate companion of his own soul. And with this discovery, the journey of flight was over and the journey of faith was begun. One of the great spiritual explorations of the human spirit was complete and from it was born this faith of the explorer:

Search me, O God, and know my heart: try me, and know my thoughts: and see if there be any wicked way in me, and lead me in the way everlasting.

II

Life being what it is, we are all explorers and we need a faith adequate for that fact. We may not be standing, as did Columbus, on the prow of a ship that sailed uncharted seas, but we can say as truly as he

We break new seas today!

We shall surely misunderstand the nature and miss the meaning of life unless we are able both to regard it as a continuous exploration into an unfolding mystery and to face its many problems with a faith akin to that of the Psalmist. The mysterious meaning of life presses in from all sides of our experience.

We move from the fairly well-known present into the quite unknown future. We may object to this fact, as many have done and continue to do, but whether we object or not, life keeps right on propelling us from the known and experienced into the un-known and unexperienced. There is no way we can turn back and no way to stand still. We have no choice about the fact itself but we can and must choose whether we shall face it with fear or faith.

This enforced exploration of the future, whether with fear or faith, is experienced in every important area of personal living. The very pattern of the life process makes it inevitable, for it ordains that life, normally, shall be conceived, born, and move from infancy to maturity to old age, and, finally, to death.

Lorado Taft, one of America's greatest sculptors, was preoccupied with this fact when he designed the magnificent piece of statuary that stands at the south end of the Midway at the University of Chicago. Spend an hour before it sometime, and you will find it a great teacher. Study the faces of the people in the vast procession that moves across the face of that stone, and you will know why the artist called it "Life." Beginning as a babe in arms, man moves through a happy, carefree childhood, a puzzled adolescence, a strong maturity, a stable old age, and finally, bowed down with years, yet with face uplifted, he moves off the canvas of stone to death itself.

While a student at the University, I used to pass this creation several times a week. Its power grew each time I studied it. It is only fair to report that I maintained and kept in good order my own private cemetery directly in front of it. There I quietly and regretfully interred many a world-shaking idea and insight and not a few plans for righting the accumulated wrongs of man in one generation. When placed in the perspective of eternity which dominates that work of art, they were stricken with a chill and died. But the notion that man needs God, needs Him above all else, needs a great faith in God as the Creator and Companion of life, received a powerful reinforcement each time I stood before it.

Most of us do not find it difficult, do we, to remember the constant tremors of alarm that came to us as we thought of leaving and finally left our parental home and went into a home of our own? And when we finally made the break, the marvel is that we did not die of homesickness! We can sympathize with the little girl who was visiting a friend and spending her first night away from home. The mother of her friend heard her sobbing quietly and asked,

"What is it, honey? Are you homesick?" "No," cried the little girl, "I'm here sick." It was hard on us to go and equally hard on our parents to let us go. I think so often of the father of a large family who had come to hate a certain train that came through the town where they lived. He had it in for that particular train because it was the one each of his children took as they left home for college or work. One morning after helping one of them on it, he stood watching it pull away, muttering to himself, "It's got another one of my boys!"

That's life: they could not help wanting to go and actually going; he could not help both wanting them to go yet hate to see them leave.

Through work, friendship and love we enter into relationships that lead in new directions, confronting us with new and difficult responsibilities. The smooth face of the child cannot help giving way to the furrowed brow of the man.

Every parent will recall the world of difference the first cry of his first child made. Quite literally it opened the door to a new world —one in which the word "responsibility" took on a new dimension of seriousness and meaning. That sound drove a division in our life that cleft it into "before and after" and we accepted that fact with joy mingled with fear. It is not at all hard to understand the reaction of a hitherto fast-stepping young man to the news that their first-born son had safely arrived. The look of relief and joy that flooded his face swiftly drained away, and he whispered more to himself than to anyone else, "I've got to settle down. I've got to settle down."

We have faced or we will face temptations and trials, disappointments and sorrows, loss and tragedy, and, at the end, death itself. They are not the whole story of life, to be sure, but they are parts of that story, and the parts that give us the greatest trouble. These experiences are doors through which we must and do walk into a future that is shot through and through with the unforeseeable, the unpredictable, the unknown. When we find life leading us through them we may well draw back with alarm, but we cannot refuse to follow. For follow we must—whether in bitterness or in trust, whether in fear or in faith.

I cannot think of anything that parents and teachers and anyone else who works with children can do for them that will prove to be of such importance throughout the entire journey of life as to help them win for themselves the faith of the explorer:

Search me, O God, and know my heart: try me, and know my thoughts: and see if there be any wicked way in me, and lead me in the way everlasting.

III

Living as we do in an era of revolutions that, for the most part, are far from finished, the ultimate end of which none of us can see plainly, we have no choice but to try to find a firm path through as perilous a future as men have ever faced. We meet the word and the fact of revolution wherever we turn: the industrial revolution, the American Revolution, the Chinese Revolution, the Russian Revolution. Two years ago Peter Drucker blandly informed us that "if you are an American and over twenty-five, you have taken part, knowingly or unknowingly, in 'one of the greatest social revolutions in history.' " [2] I am not now calling for a show of hands on whether we approve of any or all or none of these revolutions. That might be interesting but not at all useful or relevant. I am letting their number and scope underscore the simple fact that we have lived and will continue to live out our lives in as revolutionary a period as men have ever known. And the question I want to ask is this: What kind of man is best fitted for living in such an age?

The clown, the humorist, the wisecracker, the man who without any great faith of his own in anyone or anything, gets a kind of sadistic satisfaction in making fun of the faith of others? Is this the kind of man we want "to match against the world"? They remind me of the tumbleweeds we used to watch in the windstorms that swept our farm in Nebraska. The weeds, as you may know, were circular in shape and usually a foot or so in diameter

[2] *Saturday Evening Post*, Jan. 19, 1952.

before the wind could pull them loose. Then they would roll and bounce ahead of it as far as the eye could see. We loved to try to catch them and always enjoyed watching them. There are people like that—and they bear about the same relationship to these days as a tumbleweed does to a high wind. Without the rootage of responsibility and commitment anywhere in the whole range of life, they delight in measuring their usefulness in terms of the whirls they make and the distance of their bounce. They serve their best purpose in being living reminders of how life should not be lived if it is not to be wholly wasted. They have yet to learn— if they ever will learn—that it is a fairly easy thing to poke fun at the faith of others but a most exacting and difficult thing to hammer out a faith for oneself that can be matched against these days.

The self-styled realist, the "touch guy"—is he any better fitted for our times? The fellow who thinks he can dismiss the hunger of half the world with a sneer about "a pint of milk for every Hottentot"; the man who dismisses the opportunity to help India get hydroelectric dams and other essentials of modern industry because "they will compete with us, and there are too many of them anyway and the easier you make life for them the faster they will multiply"; the man who thinks that this or any other nation has the right to and can slow down and finally stop by repressive and military means the billion and a half people of Asia who are on the march toward a kind of security they have never known before and now think possible of achievement—is this the faith and are these the men best fitted to live and serve this age?

Over against that faith and these men I should like to put the faith of the Psalmist incarnate in people neither better nor wiser than we are. The man of faith in God, we hold, is best fitted to serve the present age. He will not know all the answers but he will know that he does not know the answers—and there is some advantage in that! He will believe that an answer exists, and that it can be found and that, when found, it will embrace the welfare not of just a few of us who would freeze the status quo at the point of our maximum advantage but of all men evenly and equally. He will not regard himself as infallible at any stage of his journey. He will have his own ideas as to what ought to be done in any given situation, but he will be conscious at all times that they may be wholly wrong and are surely incomplete. Therefore he will both seek and welcome the views of those who disagree with him. Hating to see old patterns of thought and life broken up, reluctant to see and share in the modification of hallowed institutions, he will nonetheless face the epochal changes taking place before our eyes and say:

> The old order changeth, yielding place to new,
> And God fulfils himself in many ways.

He can do this with freedom of mind and confidence of spirit because he knows that all ideas, plans and institutions are finally subject to the mind and will of God. To discover that will, to trust in it implicitly, to fulfill it to the best of his ability will be his "meat and drink." His daily prayer will be his daily life:

Search me, O God, and know my heart: try me, and know my thoughts: and see if there be any wicked way in me, and lead me in the way everlasting.

IV

We belong to a Church that has never stood still, despite man's best efforts to set the brakes at various times over her nineteen hundred years of existence. When Jesus said to his disciples, "Go ye into all the world and preach the gospel to every creature," he set a pattern that has guided the deepest and most creative thinking and planning of the Church from that day to this. Wesley was standing squarely in that tradition when he claimed the world for his parish and had the temerity to say to one of his preachers, George Shadford, as he sent him to America, "The time has come for you to go to America. I let you loose, George, on the great continent of America. Publish your message in the open face of the sun and do all the good you can."

The Church has always had more to fear from timidity from within her fellowship than from opposition outside it. All too frequently, instead of confronting those of "a fearful heart" with the prophetic cry, "Be strong! Your God will come and save!" she has said or seemed to say, "Let's find a place away from the main issues of life where we can crouch down and rest a while and let someone else lead out." This attitude—call it calculated prudence or sheer cowardice, as you will—has weakened but never stilled the witness of the Church to her faith in God. And it will be an evil day for man if it ever should!

The Church is breaking new seas today. With the whole world as her parish, with all the broken spirits and troubled lives of two and a half billion of men as her burden, how could it be otherwise? With our economic life periodically convulsed by conflicts between management and labor, isn't it about time the Church sets up, as she has done, ways and means of studying "The Church and economic life" and asks both management and labor to help? With one marriage in three ending in divorce, and with the traditional institution of the family seriously shaken by the tempo and requirements of modern life, is it any wonder that we are beginning to study "the Church and family life"?

Thus it goes—thus it should and must go throughout the entire range of life: the Church must lead the way and do so because of her faith in the reality of a way and her conviction that it can be found and followed by men in fellowship with one another and with God. The Church does not have the answers in these areas, but she believes that she has the men and the women who, through faith in one another and in God, can find the answers. And she cannot—dare not—rest until they are found. Nor will she let us rest unless we are looking for them!

Do not look for an end to the Crusades and Advances of our church. We dare not let them end. They are a part of the genius of our church. Better than anything else they explain the amazing growth and continuing vigor of our tradition. There is every reason to believe that successive General Conferences of The Methodist Church will be true to our heritage and come up with a stirring challenge to address ourselves with renewed vigor in new ways to the problems of our age. And we, if we are worthy heirs, will respond with high heart and steady hand.

Henry C. Link, in his last book, *The Way to Security*, says that "the fear of the future has become our most widespread and disastrous fear." That, I am sure, is true, and that is why the Church must bear so heavy a burden these days. She does not fear the future, because she believes in God and knows that our times are in His hand. If the Church is true to her gospel, she will be a center of new courage and hope in a world sadly in need of both. We are the spiritual heirs of Jesus Christ whose life and thought were in continual grip with the problems that separate man from man and man from God. We are those who through the centuries have believed that the God of the universe would "lead us in the way everlasting." One of the difficulties of being an heir is the responsibility of being an ancestor.

XIX

Enthusiasm in Religion

∿∿∿∿∿∿∿∿∿∿∿∿∿∿∿∿∿∿∿∿∿∿∿∿∿∿∿∿∿∿∿∿∿∿∿∿

Scripture Lesson: Psalm 147:1–20

I

THE last four psalms in the Psalter are psalms of praise. They radiate enthusiasm, joy, gratitude and thanksgiving. Yet, withal, they are amazingly realistic in lining up reason for their enthusiasm. The writer of the 147th Psalm gathers up some sixteen such reasons, ranging all the way from "healing the brokenhearted" to casting "forth his ice like morsels." They illustrate rather than exhaust the nature of God's loving care for His people and the motif of profound enthusiasm.

I mention this now because it stands in such vivid contrast with that dull, washed-out, faded, timid thing that all too many of us call "our religion."

Henry Sloane Coffin once said that "ours is an age that is wistful in matters of religion." Wistful and deeply troubled, too, about many things in our faith, our creeds and our practices. One such concern centers in the word "enthusiasm."

A brilliant professor at the University of California after hearing a man who was enthusiastic about his religion, said, "I'd like to get the *feel* of a faith like that." So would we all. We want to feel at home with our religion; we want to enjoy it; we want to live it in full sincerity and honesty and with as little hypocrisy as possible. Yet we draw back from its fervor, contagion and enthusiasm with real concern. And well we might because enthusiasm comes to us bearing a blessing in one hand and a curse in the other. If we are not careful she will give us both hands at the same time.

The word "enthusiasm" was born under circumstances that were prophetic of its future. Like its sister word "inspiration" it came to birth in the religious ceremonies of ancient Greece. The religious festivals of that day were quite lavish, occupying several days and the center of everyone's attention. There were songs, dramas, parades, sacrifices, food and drink. The climax of the festival was a torchlight procession to the sacred places or shrines where offerings were placed on the altar, thus, they thought, lifting the weight of sin from them and guaranteeing the favor of God.

Understandably, the worshipers experienced a sense of exhilaration, of joy, of new power and life that made them feel like quite different people. And, being Greeks, they had or coined a word— two words in fact—for it: "enthusiasm" means "God within" and "inspiration" meaning "spirit within."

This experience of joy, peace and new life was much older than the Greek word for it. In fact, it is as old and as universal as religion itself. All primitive religions make much of what we call "spirit possession"—the experience of having the power of God take possession of a man or a people. While we have sloughed off many of the cruder forms which this experience has taken and many of the bizarre explanations of it, we have not been able to devise a religion worthy of the name without it. For at the heart of vital faith, whether ancient or modern, primitive or sophisticated is an experience of God that brings joy, peace and a sense of new life to the one who experiences it.

Even so, enthusiasm in religion has always been suspect—and rightly so. It needs to carry the label: "Danger—Explosive—Handle with Care." For when enthusiasm gets out of hand it becomes a riot of emotionalism and makes havoc of life. And even when it is kept under strict control it disturbs the status quo all along the line. Let a man get on fire with his faith and strange things are bound to happen.

That, better than anything else, explains the incredible behavior of the prophets of ancient Israel: Elijah stripped down to his loin cloth running ahead of King Ahab's chariot into the city; Hosea marrying a prostitute in order to illustrate to his people God's mercy toward them; Isaiah walking the streets of Jerusalem for three days stark naked foretelling the dark days ahead when defeat would strip Jerusalem of every possession. However much the authorities—kings and priests—might struggle against these enthusiastic men, they could neither control nor silence them.

St. Francis of Assisi was an enthusiast if ever there was one! The church authorities hardly knew what to make of him or what to do with him. Some wanted to throw him out of the church; others wanted to elevate him to the papacy. He and his band of enthusiastic followers swept through the church like a cleansing fire, reawakening a sense of humble sacrificial loyalty to Jesus Christ. Long before Francis' death, the question had shifted from being "What are we going to do with him?" to "What is he going to do with us?"

Our own church, The Methodist Church, was brought into being on a wave of religious enthusiasm that stirred England as she had seldom been stirred before. The upper classes might scoff at Wesley and his preachers; learned men might pick flaws in their logic; the Established Church might close her doors to them—but the miners, the factory workers, the dock workers of England not only heard them gladly but under their leadership learned to sing, to pray and to worship God with joyous hearts.

You just do not follow the frontiers of a new country as the circuit riders did in the early days of this country unless you are an enthusiastic and inspired person. Laugh at their foibles, single out their weaknesses, deplore their excesses, if we will and must—for they were all too human and none knew it better than they. But who will deny them this simple testimony: With no expectation of ease or worldly goods as reward, they shared their faith with all who would listen, no matter what the cost? They deserve to be listed in that fellowship of early churchmen who were characterized by a self-sacrificing enthusiasm that is essential to the church. On that firm foundation we have built our church. At the center of any great man or movement we will find an overflowing love and a contagious enthusiasm that literally takes possession of life.

II

Yet the existence of even great men and movements like the ones we have been talking about should emphasize rather than blind us to the dangers of enthusiasm in religion. Granting its irreplaceable importance in religious faith, we should nonetheless be intimately acquainted with the dangers it carries. Let me, therefore, file as strong a brief as possible against enthusiasm in religion.

1. *Enthusiasm cripples our critical faculties.* When we get enthusiastic about something we tend to exclude from consideration all troublesome questions and contradictory evidence. We tend to forget the facts we do not like. We begin to associate with only those people who agree with us. Dryden, the British poet, was thoroughly soured on enthusiasts and enthusiasm when he wrote, "Truth is never to be expected from authors whose undertakings are warped with enthusiasm; for they judge all actions and causes by their own perverse principles, and a crooked line can never be the measure of a straight one."

Psychologists would agree that there is much truth in this gloomy judgment, and history surely warns us not to ignore it.

2. *Enthusiasm breeds dogmatism and cruelty.* Paul is an eloquent example of this. Raised as a Pharisee, he was zealous to defend the law against all doubters. When he went to Jerusalem he was shocked to discover the Christian group openly challenging the law. His enthusiasm leaped to the conclusion that the Christian group should be exterminated, and he volunteered to take the lead in the effort. He was so successful that he was first known throughout the Christian Church as their most relentless persecutor. Years later, looking back on all this, Paul says, "I thought I was doing God's will." So does every other religious enthusiast. Who can measure the damage done in human life by the fanaticism and bigotry that parade as legitimate enthusiasm?

Arne Garborg, Danish writer, once wrote a book entitled *Peace* that has as its central character Enok, an intensely and devotedly religious person. Enok is the father and the head of the house in the story. He wears queer clothes; he insists upon absolute quiet during meals; he forbids folk songs, secular books and worldly amusement; he insists upon indeterminable periods of Bible reading and praying; he sets himself up as an infallible authority on speech, dress and morals. And as a direct result of his cruelty—there is no other name for it—he ruins his wife's health, makes his home hell, alienates his son, and finally becomes so despondent about his own sinfulness that he commits suicide.

Nor is Garborg the only one to protest against the ease with which enthusiasm slips over into fanaticism, bigotry and simple cruelty in human relations. Sir Edmund Gosse grew up in a home of devout evangelical parents who tried to guide their life by the rigid and unyielding tenets of their faith. The boy rebelled against it when he became a young man and later he wrote one of the most eloquent indictments of enthusiasm in religion I have ever read:

Let me speak plainly. After my long experience, after my patience and forbearance, I have surely the right to protest against the untruth (would that I could apply to it any other word!) that evangelical religion, or any religion in a violent form, is a wholesome or valuable or desirable adjunct to human life. It divides heart from heart. It sets up a vain, chimerical ideal in the barren pursuit of which all the tender, indulgent affections, all the genial play of life, all the exquisite pleasures and soft resignations of the body, all that enlarges and calms the soul, are exchanged for what is harsh and void and negative. It encourages a stern and ignorant spirit of condemnation; it throws altogether out of gear the healthy movement of the conscience; it invents virtues which are sterile and cruel; it invents sins which are no sins at all, but which darken the heaven of innocent joy with futile clouds of remorse. There is something horrible, if we will bring ourselves to face it, in the fanaticism that can do nothing with this pathetic and fugitive existence of ours but treat it as if it were the uncomfortable antechamber to a palace which no one has explored and of the plan of which we know absolutely nothing. My Father, it is true, believed that he was intimately acquainted with the form and furniture of this habitation, and he wished me to think of nothing else but of the advantages of an eternal residence in it.[1]

3. A third indictment of enthusiasm is this: *It can gather a crowd and weld that crowd into a mob.*

I am not now referring to what the late President Charles William Eliot of Harvard once called the "autumn madness" that strikes colleges and universities and is localized in the stadium! That I regard as a thoroughly enjoyable experience.

But if you remember hearing the booming *"Sieg Heils"* of the Nuremburg Congress of the Nazi party in the late thirties, you know what I mean. And every skillful propagandist knows what I mean, too! The problem of propaganda is not to keep people from thinking or to encourage them to think creatively; it is to encourage them to think about one or two things and then to whip their enthusiasm to a frenzy.

III

Yet—a powerful case can be built *for* enthusiasm—one we tend to overlook.

1. *To begin with, enthusiasm is natural:* We are creatures of feeling, of emotion, of desires, fears, and all the rest. We cannot live without our emotions no matter how much trouble we may have with them. Simply to live is to be moved or influenced by someone or something that appeals to us, that we want or like or believe in. Pure objectivity is a myth as far as we are concerned. We do more than think about ideas; we believe, we feel, we know, we hate, we love. Quite obviously any significant interest or activity whether in science or art or patriotism or religion is going to appeal to our emotions. Enthusiasm, then, is no alien creation of religion imported into the human enterprise for the purpose of confusing us; it is at home with man and has always been. Much as we may deplore its ravages and excesses, we neither can nor would wish to disown it throughout life.

2. *Enthusiasm is not only natural, it is essential to any great*

[1] Gosse, *Father and Son*, Scribner's, 1921, pp. 302-3.

effort or achievement. Emerson, about as cold-blooded a thinker as we have ever produced in the life of our country, was exactly right when he said, "Every great and commanding movement in the annals of the world is the triumph of enthusiasm—nothing great was ever accomplished without it." Even a sober treatise on ethics comes up with this gem, "No virtue is safe that is not enthusiastic."

We see this early enough in creative citizenship. A good citizen is one who begins with a passionate love for his country—an enthusiasm for her life, culture and institutions that is all the more creative because it is sincerely alert to the unsolved problems and unmet needs in the life of the people. He will level his criticisms at his country, but they will always be set in the context of his love for, and loyalty to, that country. He will not pull a Garry Davis and try to live as a man without a country. To do that is merely to shift the problems of citizenship to the shoulders of someone else.

The artist must love his work, must be enthusiastic about it, must give himself to it wholeheartedly if he is going to probe to the depths of its meaning for his life and be able to share it with anyone else. As you get acquainted with the life of any great artist you seem to hear this overtone, "I have something to say that needs to be said; I am the one to say it and I intend to say it as best I can as long as I live."

Religion is a way of life. Even more, it is a challenge to live a kind of life that far transcends the one we now live. As such, it must excite interest, arouse enthusiasm, and secure sacrificial commitment. Objectivity has its place in religion, to be sure, but not the kind of objectivity which we find in this title of a sixteenth-century book: *The Ultimate Profession of Faith of Simon Sinai of Lucca, first Roman Catholic, then Calvinist, then Lutheran, then again Catholic, but always an atheist.*

As a way of life and a way toward a new life, religion suggests goals and purposes for us and commends them to us. It urges us to believe in, strive for, and if necessary die for certain great ends. It invites us to share in the life of the Christian Church which is supposed to be a group where contagious enthusiasm for, and loyalty to, the ends of religious faith are fundamental. We do not know as much as we would like to know about the great figures in the early Church, but we possess enough information about Philip to admire the zeal, the enthusiasm and the tireless way in which he went about his work. I might as well confess it—Philip was a churchman after my heart.

Forced to flee from Jerusalem with the Christian group until a wave of persecution had passed, he went straight to Samaria where any Jew who sought to preach was sure of a rough reception. He met the challenge head-on, and successfully. By dint of hard work he was able to bring into being the nucleus of a strong church. This he turned over to others for continuing leadership while he headed south—looking for new fields to plow. He found them "on a desert road" and in the person of a richly decked out messenger of a royal house in Egypt. The messenger was reading from one of the scrolls of sacred scripture as the chariot moved along. Philip was nothing if not an opportunist. He asked what has always struck me as an impertinent question, "Do you understand what you are reading?" And, before Philip hopped out of the chariot, the man had professed conversion, arranged for his own baptism in a roadside pool, and was ready to go on his way rejoicing. It was of Philip and a thousand others like him that one of our most reliable historians was writing when he said,

A tempestuous enthusiasm, an overwhelming intensity of feeling, an immediate awareness of the presence of God, an incomparable sense of power and an irresistible control over the will and inner spirit and even the physical conditions of other men—these are ineradicable features of historic early Christianity." [2]

IV

Enthusiasm and great religion go hand in hand. How could it be otherwise if we are to take seriously the ideal of a Christian life, a Christian society and a Christian Church? These are not merely

[2] Johaness Weiss, The History of Primitive Christianity, Vol. I, They Upset the World! Wilson and Erickson, 1937, pp. 42–43.

words to be uttered or far-off goals to be praised; they are problems to be accepted, studied and solved as best we can here and now. Yet enthusiasm, to be creative, must be sincere; it cannot be pretended; it must drive its roots to the very heart of our thinking and our living. We cannot turn it on and off as we do a spigot. Jesus' formula for engendering enthusiasm continues to be the only one that is adequate to the task. He said we must learn to love God with our whole being and our neighbor as ourself. Then, he continued, we will be ready for the great commandment of taking the gospel to the ends of the earth. Creative enthusiasm roots in a vision of the meaning of life and of our responsibility for accepting and implementing that vision with our life. That, I am sure, is why sacrifice is always linked with enthusiasm in the Christian faith.

The case for enthusiasm, I suppose, might be summarized by contrasting it with its opposite number in the scale of human attitudes. Enthusiasm's opposite number is not objectivity as some think; it is apathy, indifference, insensitivity. That, I greatly fear, is the state in which citizenship and churchmanship are usually found. A country of apathetic citizens is a weak, irresolute country and headed for some form of dictatorship as certainly as the sun rises. A church composed of apathetic members is on its way out and will be replaced by another that is blessed with a contagious enthusiasm throughout its fellowship.

We like enthusiastic people. We do not like apathetic people. We like enthusiastic groups. We do not like apathetic groups. And we react as we do either because we share their enthusiasm or envy them it.

A wise old minister was once confronted with this question by a group of young men going into the ministry, "How do you begin working on your sermon?" He answered, "Get on fire with it— that's the only place you can begin." You begin more than a sermon there, you begin great churchmanship there. For it is excellent advice for all churchmen to "get on fire with your churchmanship." Learn to love the church for her message, her mission, her program. Let your love become the basis for a contagious enthusiasm for the church. Then you will be a good churchman not only of the church as she is but of the church as she ought to be. Like Philip of old in the New Testament story you will take advantage of any and every opportunity to share your love and your loyalty to the church with others.

Are you as disturbed as I am by the fact that half the adult citizens of this country have no overt interest in the program of religious institutions? Are you searching, as I am, for some effective answer that can be given to this problem that demands solution in our common life? Do you share with me the conviction that the only effective answer to apathy is enthusiasm, that the only convincing answer to apathetic churchmanship is enthusiastic churchmanship?

If we are agreed in this, then, let us make a covenant now that so far as in us lies, we personally are going to become centers of contagious enthusiasm for this church, the church universal, and the Christian faith which lies at the heart of our church. Let us make a love of the church and enthusiasm for the church and a sacrificial loyalty to the church essential parts of all that we think, say and do. As we do this and to the extent that we are able to do it, there will come into existence here in our common life a sense of joy, peace and new life that deserves the ancient word "God within."

XX

Art in Religion

wwwwwwwwwwwwwwwwwwwwwwwwwwwwwwwwwwwwwwwwwwwwwwwwww

SCRIPTURE LESSON: Psalm 149:1–5; 150:1–6

I

FROM time immemorial, art and religion, like true lovers, have alternately fought and embraced each other. This hectic relationship will doubtless continue until we accept the fact that they are inseparable aspects of human life. As long as we are going to have culture and civilization in any recognizable form, we shall have both art and religion. If we make cultural progress, it will be reflected in both disciplines. The two cannot be separated though there are those among us who proclaim the divorce. The history of mankind is dotted with efforts to effect such a separation, yet each time art and religion have given them the lie by flowing together again. We have reason to be grateful for the fact that in our time this flowing-together process is at flood tide. It is going on in churches the world over, and it ought to be going on in each one of us who seeks to be a creative member of our religious tradition. This can happen only as we are able to appreciate the role which art has played in religion.

We need to begin with the simple fact that art and religion have enjoyed periods of very intimate harmony. They have never been closer together than they were in primitive culture. They were then so close as to be indistinguishable from each other. There were no such things as art and religion separate and distinct from each other. They were part and parcel of everything that happened in the life of the people. The great tribal feasts and dances were both art and religion, as we understand those terms now. For example, the ceremonial dance of a certain people was held in a secluded spot where the eyes of aliens and strangers could not behold the sacred rites. Here they met and chanted their ancestral songs, recited the legends of their fathers, wore appropriate garments, danced about the totem pole on which were carved likenesses of their god or gods. If, perchance, upon this occasion they were celebrating the deliverance of their fathers from famine, a drama was certain to be enacted. Some of the participants would drop to the ground feigning death from starvation. Others would run feebly about looking everywhere for food. Suddenly, the hero of the tribe would appear bringing food. Then the dead would spring up from the ground, the weakening ones would revive, and the dance would whirl on to a triumphant climax. This is art. But it is also religion. It is art because they dance, they sing, they dramatize, they adorn, they carve, and they paint. And it is religion because it catches up the living persons, reunites them with their past, consecrates them to a new sense of fellowship with one another, and strengthens them for their task.

It is no derogation of modern religious services to point out that they have recognizable connections with early religious ceremony. Our secluded place is the church, or the cathedral; we meet here as a body; we read from our Scriptures; in some churches, we have likenesses of divine beings; most churches have vestments which set apart the officiaries; we dramatize the experience of God and of man meeting God in our ritual. This is religion, profound religion, we say. It is likewise art, and, if properly done, it can be great art.

II

The Hebrew tradition in which we share in so many fundamental ways made a wide but quite uneven use of art. It rejected some art forms altogether, notably sculpturing and what might be called the art of personal and public adornment. Why this aversion? you ask. The Hebrews were deathly afraid of idols, images or any graven or carved likeness of man or God. It was a sacrilege, they thought, and they would have none of it. But they did make wide and free use of various other art forms. The simple architecture of their early temples gradually became more ornate and eloquent in the later ones. They used the song, the dance, and all forms of instrumental music in their temple liturgies and folk festivals. They used poetry and chants, or Psalms set to music, in the stately services of worship in temple and synagogue. The Psalms read earlier in the service today make it abundantly plain that the early Hebrews, as well as the later ones, turned to such art forms with spontaneous joy as well as deepest reverence.

The early Christians, being Jews, followed this ancestral pattern of art forms quite closely. But, from the outset, the Christians faced a serious problem. Surrounded as they were and preaching to idol-loving Greeks and Romans, they thundered against idols, idol worship, and everything connected with them. Since Greek and Roman drama were based upon the legends of pagan religion, the Christian preachers rejected the Greek and Roman theaters and the rich dramatic traditions of Aeschylus, Sophocles and Euripides. It is fair to say that they held in sharp suspicion any evidence that anyone was enjoying life, and under their influence the happy dances of earlier peoples subsided into silent processionals, and the vivacious folk songs that used to be spontaneous shouts of joy became sober chants. But these ancient arts did not die easily nor did they conform readily to the lines laid down by the early Christian preachers. They kept on stirring among early Christians until these prohibitions were either modified or removed. Then they burst forth in radiant expression once more. Instead of plain meeting houses the great basilicas and cathedrals came into existence. The early chants gave way to Palestrina and to later geniuses of the musical tradition of the Church. The folk festivals all over Europe once more were infected (if that is the word we want) and they became religious ceremonials. The Christian drawings in the catacombs of Rome, so rich in religious symbolism, do but foreshadow the later artists like Michelangelo, Da Vinci and Dürer.

You may have heard the thirteenth century presented as "The Great Century" of the Christian tradition. And indeed by any manner of reckoning, it is one of the greatest we have had. For in it there was a profound fusion of art and religion such as we had not seen before nor have we seen since. It was the age when the great cathedrals were built, when Dante's *Divine Comedy* was written, and when Thomas Aquinas' *Summa Theologica* was put in final form. All these must be regarded as ways of preaching the one and the same Gospel, not by word of mouth, not simply in logical form, but by means of every artistic medium known to man.

I do not know how you feel about it, but I never see one of these historic cathedrals without sensing in it and in the impulses that built it not alone the unity between art and religion but also the parent-unity between religion and the whole of life. The architects drew the plans. The church officials and the community accepted them. The peasants hewed out the slabs of stone and dragged them to the site of the cathedral. The artisans fitted them in their proper place. Safely there, the artists went to work giving them a richness of symbolism that continues to speak. Masons, wood carvers, glass-staining experts—all of these and many other laborers whose labor is a work of art were called upon to dedicate their skill on the altar of religion in the building of the cathedral. Perhaps the matter might be put this way: Dante's pen, Thomas' mind, the architect's skill, the mason's trowel, the people's hope and laborers—all these were consecrated to religion. Who will be so bold as to try to separate the art from the religion that went into this creation? So it went from one end of Europe to the other during "The Great Century." Stand in the presence of one of these great works of art, and you will sense the fact that if a man is going to say something religiously, he will want to say it with his whole life and with the entire range of his artistic expression.

III

Strange as it may seem, one of the most spectacular of all conflicts between art and religion came on the heels of "the great century" with the Renaissance. The fifteenth and sixteenth centuries saw a burst of the artistic spirit which knew no bounds. Men became interested in the classics of ancient Greece and Rome, and under the spur of this interest brought into existence some of our most exquisite art forms. They were less convinced by the Church than they had been previously and paid considerably less attention to the ethical admonitions of the Church. Since the morality of the day was based upon religious sanction, the morals of the people decayed with the decay of their interest in religion. Read a book like Ralph Roeder's *The Man of the Renaissance*, and you get an excellent description of how flabby the age became. It is only fair to say that many of the Popes of that period were more interested in having artists than saints in their courts.

Savonarola, a mystical monk in Florence, beheld this decline in morals with great alarm. He preached against it with such vigor and effectiveness that he was reckoned the foremost preacher of his time. He was feared and respected by Pope and king alike, even though he did not exert any great influence on their behavior. He succeeded in getting control of the civil authority in Florence, and when he did, he set about cleaning up the situation there. One of the first things he did was to collect all of the classics he could find and have a great bonfire in the public square of the city. It was his dramatic way of saying that the new interest in art had undercut morality and that the only way to re-establish morality was to destroy art. But Savonarola was a strayed ghost of an earlier age, and the currents of his day soon swept his influence away. There came another day when there was another fire in the public square of Florence. This time Savonarola was burned.

Our Puritan ancestors had more than a full-sized grudge against art; they carried on a full-sized war against it, too. Vernon Louis Parrington's *Main Currents in American Thought* has detailed this story in an unforgettable way. Reacting as they did against the rigidity of the form and the laxity of the morals of the Royal Court and the English Church, the Puritans denounced both immorality and formalism with equal vigor. They resolved to make their services of worship the acme of simplicity—and they succeeded. Vestments, ritual, liturgy and ornate buildings were taboo. When the Puritans seized civil power, they closed the theater forthwith as an instrument of the Devil. We might note in passing that they closed it so effectively that the theater did not really regain its power for a hundred years! The churches in New England today continue to show traces of this early austerity. Whether you stand in the First Baptist Church of Providence, Rhode Island, or in the lovely Memorial Church of Harvard University, you sense the fact that these buildings are simplicity itself. They are rectangular in shape; they are constructed of plain stone or wood. For the most part the windows are still made of clear glass, though here and there stained glass is beginning to testify to a compromise with early Puritan custom. Much of the criticism which is leveled against churches that strive for a wider use of all art forms today continues to come from those who either have not taken the trouble to re-examine their Puritan heritage or who, having done so, continue to believe it valid in its attempt to separate art and religion.

IV

This much history states with assurance: art and religion cannot long be separated. They are too deeply interdependent. When they are separated, both suffer. Working together both thrive. Separated, they weaken and wither. United, they extend the range of each other's work and witness. Even in their bitterest conflicts, they remind one of weary wrestlers who lean upon each other even as they are struggling together. Savonarola used the art of persuasion to depreciate art. The Puritans developed the arts of simplicity to show up the art of ornateness. And so it goes. One of the most convincing evidences of the interdependence of art and religion is to be found in the relationship between the Church and the theater, between religion and drama.

After a fitful and tragic separation which began about the year A.D. 300 the dramatic impulse sought and found expression in the mystery, miracle and morality plays all over medieval Europe. When these plays came into existence, they were very simple and forthright in their message, content and mode of presentation. Soon the dramatic impulse which fired them spread beyond them and the secular drama came into existence. When the secular drama began to mature, it became less and less interested in religious preachments, less and less interested in the religious morality which had fostered it. The secular theater turned toward the classics of Greece and Rome for themes and developed them in ways that were thoroughly shocking to the conscience of religiously-minded people. The theater ridiculed the Church and the Church denounced the theater. When the theater had the support and the protection of the state, it was safe. When the Church was able to influence laws, the theater had a bad time of it. We cannot study that period when Church and theater were locked in a mortal struggle with each other without realizing that even as religion had lost the use of one of her most effective art forms, the theater had lost one of its most important functions. Both were impoverished beyond description because of that separation.

Now, in our time, drama and religion are groping toward each other once more. Thornton Wilder's play, *The Skin of Our Teeth*, T. S. Eliot's play, *Murder in the Cathedral*, and Christopher Fry's various plays, notably *The Sleep of Prisoners*, are examples of this trend. These artists do more, much more, than merely hold a mirror up to nature. They do that, to be sure, they let us see ourselves as we are, but in addition, they bring the self we are under the judgment of the self God intends us to be. And that is never a pleasant experience.

As Peter, in *The Sleep of Prisoners*, asks, "What's man to be?" David answers, "Content and full." Peter muses over that for a moment, then rejoins, "That's modest enough. What an occupation for eternity!" Once more in an insight like this we feel the sting of the artist who is trying to preach the gospel not simply in logical form, but by means of imaginative insight into the problems we face. And those of us who preach the gospel in more traditional form accept as from God the assistance of men like Christopher Fry and T. S. Eliot.

Art and religion appeal to the same kind of personalities. Each one needs a sensitive spirit before it can get its message across with any degree of emphasis. A dull-souled person makes neither a good artist nor a prophetic religionist. One of the tragedies of the last five hundred years is the way sensitive spirits who have given their

lives to art have been persecuted by slow-witted religionists. And
it works the other way too. Amateurs in art make no end of fun of
any one of their number who happens to be religious. And so the
merry whirl of calculated injustice continues.

Why are art and religion inseparable? The reason can be given
in two sentences, I believe. Religion gives great art its subject
matter. Art gives this subject matter its most eloquent formulation.
Religion points out the issues of life, the problems and situations
that break men's souls. Art deals with these issues and problems
with a depth and richness of imaginative insight that makes them
pulse with both immediate and eternal meanings. You must be
hypnotized, as I am, by the expressions on the faces of the Four
Horsemen of the Apocalypse and their victims in the famous
painting of them. Study those expressions intently the next time
you stand before the canvas, and you will get a much clearer idea
of what Famine, Pestilence, War and Death mean to mankind.
Notice especially the maddening, mocking sneer on the face of the
Fourth Horseman as he swings his scythe. What has the artist done
in this masterpiece? He has borrowed the imagery and the faith of
the book of Revelation, to be sure, but more—he has taken the
age-old experience of mankind with these scourges and he has
crystallized it into an expression on the faces of these figures. He
has given a dimension of depth to the tragic experiences of individuals, a universal and eternal expression.

This is art, great art. It is likewise religion, great religion.
For religion through the centuries has been wrestling with these
problems. Religion has tried to make crops a dead certainty and
so prevent famine. Religion has tried to cope with sickness and so
prevent pestilence. Religion has always protested against the inhumanity of war; and religion alone has endeavored to mediate when
the moment of death draws near to man. Religion has made these
themes lofty; it has lifted them to the very doors of Heaven. That
is, religion aided by the arts has done this.

You have all seen the famous picture of Jesus and the Rich
Young Ruler. Have you noticed how the artist contrasts them?
Not by the kind of tunic, nor by stature, nor by facial expression.

The world which yawns between the selfishness of the Rich Young Ruler and the selflessness of Jesus is described in the posture of their hands. Jesus' hands are open—in the posture of giving. The Rich Young Ruler's hands are closed—in the posture of getting and keeping. Only a great artist can so tellingly depict that world of difference. Such an artist is great not only because he has skill of line and pigment at his control, but even more because he has learned from religion the awful difference between selfishness and selflessness. Religion furnishes the soul of the picture; art the body.

We are fortunate in having in our sanctuary and chapel as rich a repository of various art forms as we can find anywhere in this country. We have here in the windows of these two transepts, the parables of the Gospels and various other teachings of Jesus. Undoubtedly, these teachings have been used as the basis for sermons from this pulpit since the church was built in 1911, and I am certain they will continue to be so used. Preacher after preacher will try to tie this into life a hundred different ways. That is his job. But when the sermon is over and the service is at an end, the gospel continues to be preached by these windows.

The purpose of services of worship and sanctuaries for worship was never better described than by Browning's line in "Saul":

> Thou hast done now with the eyes for the actual;
> begin with the seer's!

Worship aims to transcend the ordinary patterns of life which we follow from day to day. We get in the habit of seeing things a certain way, of doing them a certain way. We get so set in this particular way of living that it never occurs to us that there might be another and a better way. Worship aims to give us a new vista on the meaning of life. It tries to open our eyes that we may see the dimension of depth, beauty and meaning in the world round about us. We go through life like the Scottish farmer who had trampled under foot the heather of his native country without ever once thinking about it. One day Robert Burns came by and picking up a sprig of heather pointed out the exquisite finery of it. The farmer said, "And to think I've been walking on it all my life." Worship aims to hold up that which we have come to regard as commonplace and reveals its eternal meaning. It invites us to plunge beneath the surface of daily chatter and clatter, and to lay hold on the basic principles of life once more.

Balzac, a French writer, after spending an evening with friends who talked about everything in general and nothing of significance, went to his study when he got home, took off his coat, rubbed his hands, and regarding the books of the masters on the shelves, cried, "Now for some real people!" Worship is always urging us toward a richer experience of real things, real people, and real ideas. This, then, in a sentence, is the purpose of worship: to free us from our enslavement to the commonplace, to the habitual, and to give us another chance to grasp the beauty and the richness of life.

Yet as we gather together here for purposes of public worship, we make extensive use of the art forms that have expressed the meaning of religion through the ages, and were it not for them, our services would be incredibly impoverished. It is my sincere hope that every member of our church, every friend of the church, will take advantage of the opportunity we have of worshiping in this sanctuary and of becoming intimately acquainted with its manifold meaning. As we do we will be eternally grateful for the generations before us to work for and plan to bring into existence the many ways in which the Gospel is being preached here: through the wood carving on the reredos here and in the chapel; through the lovely windows of the church; through the leaping lines and the rich musical notes that add life and meaning to our sanctuary. Coming to church and sharing in the service of worship is not simply coming together to sing, to pray, and to hear the minister preach a sermon; it is entering into a place wherein one clear focus are the many lights that have been brought into existence by the creative interests of men over thousands of years. And they are focused upon us—each one of us—in this service of worship. It is as though the ages were speaking to us with a single voice!

Sir Christopher Wren was buried in St. Paul's—the cathedral

which he had designed. He asked that this epitaph be put on his monument: "If you would see his monument, look about you." And in the same spirit we might well say, If you would see the greatest memorial to those who have preceded us in our religious tradition, look about you. You do not see art here and religion there, separated from each other. You hear the voice of God speaking to you through the joint creations of art and religion. And this is as it should be since both are from God.

Set in Linotype Electra
Format by Katharine Sitterly
Manufactured by The Haddon Craftsmen, Inc.
Published by HARPER & BROTHERS, *New York*